On Aquinas

On Aquinas

HERBERT McCABE OP

Edited and Introduced
by Brian Davies OP

continuum

Published by Burns & Oates
A Continuum imprint
The Tower Building
11 York Road
London SE1 7NX

80 Maiden Lane
Suite 704,
New York NY 10038

www.continuumbooks.com

First published 2008

British Library Cataloguing-in-Publication Data
A catalogue record for this book is available from the British Library.

ISBN-13 9780860124610 (paperback)
ISBN-10 0860124614 (paperback)

Typeset by BookEns Ltd.
Printed and bound by MPG Books Ltd, Bodmin, Cornwall

Contents

Foreword

Herbert McCabe was one of the most talented English-speaking philosophers of the twentieth century. Had he chosen to pursue a conventional academic career as a philosopher – something that his friends find hard to imagine – he would quickly have risen to the top of the profession. But instead he lived the life of a Dominican friar, and so his philosophical insights were not widely shared outside the circle of his religious brethren. It is very good that now, after his death, they are being made available to a wider public.

The lectures presented in this volume were delivered as an introduction to the thought of St Thomas Aquinas. But they present a highly personal interpretation of the Saint, and contain many original and unexpected developments of his ideas.

In the English speaking world it is possible to identify four schools among contemporary admirers of Aquinas.

First, there are the conservatives who continue to work in the neo-scholastic tradition of Gilson and Maritain, albeit in a chastened and less triumphalist form. A doughty exponent of this school of thought is Ralph McInerny, who has sought to make Thomism accessible in many works.

Second, there are the transcendental Thomists who combine close and sympathetic appreciation of the writings of St Thomas with a respect for the importance of the critical insights of Immanuel Kant. Prominent leaders of this line of thought were the Jesuits Joseph Marechal and Peter Hoenen, and at the present time the school is represented above all by followers of the late Bernard Lonergan S.J.

Third, there are those who follow an agenda drawn from post-modernism, among whom are the members of the theological movement that styles itself "Radical Orthodoxy." John Milbank and Catherine Pickstock are vociferous proponents of this tendency, which has gained influence in the Church of England.

Finally, there are several philosophers in the analytic tradition, who seek to interpret Aquinas in the light of recent currents of thought in philosophy of language and philosophy of mind. Many of these have been heavily influenced by Wittgenstein, who like Aquinas stands at the opposite pole of philosophy from the Cartesian tradition which sees epistemology as the basic philosophical discipline and private consciousness as the fundamental datum of epistemology. There is by now an impressive corpus of works of this so-called analytical Thomism. Some of the leading practitioners are Catholics, such as Peter Geach and John Finnis; but there have been other influential writers of this school who – like Norman Kretzmann – have never been Catholics or – like Alasdair McIntyre – have held varying religious allegiance.

Herbert McCabe was often identified as a member of this school - an analytical Thomist. But he hated being called a Thomist of any kind, and his own spoken and written presentations of the Saint's teaching always bore a highly personal mark. He was indeed an admirer of Wittgenstein, and he sought to graft the insights of the twentieth-century thinker on to those of the thirteenth-century thinker not out of a desire to appear up to date - he showed no inclination to endorse any of the trendy intellectual fashions of the age – but because he recognized a genuine affinity between the two masters.

Undoubtedly, Aquinas and Wittgenstein shared a conviction that it is through an unconstrained attention to the operation of language that we achieve philosophical understanding. But McCabe's Aquinas is, as he admits, in a sense more linguistic than the historical Aquinas was. Whereas Aquinas himself undoubtedly believed that every thought we have can, in principle, be expressed in language, he did not, McCabe says, fully grasp that human thought just *is* the capacity to use language. "*We* analyse understanding and thinking in terms of human communication, whereas *Aquinas* analyses communication in terms of understanding and thinking".

The present book concentrates on Aquinas' philosophical anthropology – on the nature of animal and human life, on the relation between the senses and the intellect, and on the virtues that are essential to human flourishing. While McCabe makes copious use of the Aristotelian metaphysical structures that Aquinas employs, he writes in an admirably informal manner far removed from the style of the crabbed textbooks of seminary Thomism. He is more generous than Aquinas was in providing concrete examples to illustrate conceptual points, and his examples are always fresh and vivid, and are commonly convincing. They are also often surprising, as when he lists Brunel, Dictionary Murray, Lenin, and Bob Geldof as examples of the virtue of *magnanimitas*.

Though the book will appeal especially to those who are already aware of the abiding value of Aquinas' insights, it could serve very well as a general introduction to the philosophy of human nature. The book is not a treatise about Aquinas, it is an exercise in philosophy with Aquinas.

Introduction

Since his death in 2001 it has been my privilege to edit and prepare for publication a substantial amount of unpublished material left behind by Herbert McCabe OP. Readers, therefore, now have available (all under an imprint of Continuum) *God Still Matters* (2002), *God, Christ and Us* (2003), *The Good Life* (2005), and *Faith Within Reason* (2007). These volumes, which have received extremely favourable reviews, provide a vivid sense of McCabe's personality and cast of mind. They illustrate how deep Christian sensibility can be combined with rigorous philosophical argument. They show us how it is indeed possible skilfully to display what St Anselm of Canterbury famously referred to as 'faith seeking understanding'.

One reason they do so lies in the fact that McCabe was very much a student and defender of Thomas Aquinas. It would be wrong to say that McCabe was a 'Thomist' since, with good reason, he took Thomism to be a relatively recent phenomenon, one often at odds with what Aquinas himself had to say. Aquinas, McCabe frequently asserted, was not himself a Thomist. Yet McCabe was always fascinated by things that Aquinas wrote, and the influence of Aquinas is to be seen everywhere in his writings. Arguably, Aquinas is the most distinguished example of a Christian author pursuing the path of 'faith seeking understanding', which is why McCabe's writings are what they are—a series of brilliant essays using serious philosophy in the service of theology, a collection of texts in which central Christian themes are thought through and engaged with as items which ought to be of interest to everyone.

Yet McCabe never published a book on Aquinas. He occasionally wrote about Aquinas, and he lectured on Aquinas's thought for several decades. But he never gave us a full-scale study of Aquinas, and I have always lamented this fact. In recent years there has been an astonishing revival of interest in Aquinas, and McCabe undoubtedly had the ability to forward this along at book length. Had he settled down to writing a volume on Aquinas, the result, I think, would have been recognized as one of the most distinguished in the field. One of McCabe's great talents when it comes to Aquinas was an ability to present the latter's thinking freshly, as important and as coming from an intelligent contemporary. Book-length studies of Aquinas often fail to do this. All too often they seem not to grasp where Aquinas's genius lies. Frequently, they provide detailed and plodding accounts of what Aquinas said but fail to engage with it critically or to make illuminating connections between the thought of Aquinas and that of later writers. Frequently, also, they do not give us a sense of why Aquinas might be exciting to read for oneself. A book on Aquinas from McCabe, I am certain, would not have had these deficiencies.

Still, he never wrote such a book. A few years before he died, however, he delivered a two-term series of lectures on Aquinas at Blackfriars, Oxford, and the present volume contains the text of these, presented as a series of chapters. McCabe never spoke publicly without a written text. So, apart from some editorial modifications and additions (e.g. the creation of chapter titles and the supplying of various references), what follows is pretty much what he said when giving the lectures. As you will see, McCabe was anything but a dry, stuffy, or unintelligible lecturer. He spoke clearly, conversationally, and colloquially. He did not presume a great deal of background knowledge on the part of his audience. And he frequently illustrated his themes with familiar examples.

I believe that the lectures contained in this book were originally advertised under some such title as 'An Introduction to Aquinas'. And this is what the text of the lectures looks like at the outset—for it begins with a brief account of Aquinas's life and reception. As McCabe continued writing, however, he clearly lost interest (if he ever had any) in providing an overview of Aquinas's thinking. Instead, he allowed himself to focus on some key theses of Aquinas of especial interest to him at the time—in particular, the nature of human action and thinking, and the question of how to live well. As he proceeded, McCabe also frequently embarked on sustained philosophical reflection of his own, though always presuming that aspects of value in Aquinas's thinking provide the context for such reflection. For these reasons I have given this volume the simple title *On Aquinas*, which is accurate without promising more than is delivered. Those who would like to read McCabe on aspects of Aquinas not treated here might like to check the following: *Law, Love and Language* (London, 1968; repr. Continuum, 2003); 'A Sermon for St Thomas', in *God Matters* (London, 1987; repr. Continuum, 2005); 'The Logic of Mysticism', 'Aquinas on the Trinity', and 'Aquinas on the Incarnation', in *God Still Matters*; and 'A Very Short Introduction to Aquinas' and 'Aquinas on "God is Good"', in *Faith Within Reason*.

I should note in conclusion that, except when otherwise indicated, quotations from Aquinas are translated by McCabe himself. I should also express thanks to Victor Austin, for turning an exceedingly messy set of typescripts into an electronic version on which I could work for editorial purposes, to Timothy Bartel, for an excellent job of copy-editing, and to Christopher Upham, for help with proofreading.

Brian Davies OP
Fordham University
New York

Chapter 1

Aquinas Himself

If you want to place Aquinas historically, think of him as living for about half a century almost exactly in the middle of the thirteenth century. He was born in what we now call Italy and at a time when the politics of that region were dominated by the endless conflict between the Pope and the Emperor down in the south. Thomas's family, for part of the time anyway, were on the Emperor's side against the Pope. One of the things the half-Christian Emperor Frederick had done was to found the new University of Naples, which was set up to train his civil servants in conscious and deliberate opposition to the papal-chartered universities of Paris and Bologna. Being in the south of Italy, it was in constant communication with the Islamic civilization of the Mediterranean, a culture immensely more sophisticated in those days than anything yet available in Christian Europe.

It is not surprising then to find that Thomas was sent at the age of about fifteen to this new university. You went to a university much younger in those days—as soon as you acquired a fairly elementary education and, of course, were fluent enough in Latin to converse with and learn from people from all over the place with different languages of their own.

At the university two things happened to him at this impressionable age which clearly determined the rest of his life. First of all he met an Irishman called Peter (Petrus Hibernicus), who introduced him to some bewildering and exciting new thinking that was filtering in from Islamic sources. A whole lot of texts of Aristotle were beginning to make their way through Naples into Europe, texts that nobody there had seen before.

Aristotle, a student and critical disciple of Plato, and a teacher of Alexander of Macedon, was a marine biologist who not only observed and classified his specimens but used the same methods in all sorts of other areas like physics, astronomy, the study of society, and of what makes human beings tick. He found time to invent logic in its modern sense, and moreover was intensely interested in what we would nowadays call philosophy of science—questions about what it means to pursue such studies, and questions about language itself and so on. Medieval Europe was being quite suddenly hit by systematic scientific investigation and thinking. Many of Aristotle's *answers* turned out to be wrong, but that didn't matter. It was the method that mattered. This is what the young Aquinas encountered and fell in love with. One outstanding feature of it all was that it seemed completely subversive of Christianity, especially as it came through Christendom's main enemy, Islam. This didn't worry the Emperor too much but it must have presented an exciting challenge to Thomas. Anyway he spent much of his life painstakingly showing that if you found Aristotle right, broadly speaking, that didn't mean you had to stop being a Christian; and indeed it sometimes helped you to express the Gospel.

That interested Thomas because of the other thing that happened to him in Naples. He discovered a house with half a dozen students in it who were banded together and calling themselves 'preaching brethren'. They had come there to discover the new learning precisely in order to preach the Gospel and also to get new recruits. They were what we nowadays call the Dominicans. Thomas found them and their life—in those days rather austere, casually communal, demo-cratic—very appealing. So much so that after his studies at

Naples he told his family he wanted to be one of these preaching brethren—which was rather like a son of a Tory landowner in the eighteenth century telling, say, Squire Weston (in Henry Fielding's novel *Tom Jones*) that he wanted to be a Methodist field-preacher. There was an almighty row. They didn't mind him becoming a priest (he was evidently never going to be of much use on the battlefield), but that meant a proper priest and preferably, say, eventually the Abbot of Monte Cassino; but this begging friar thing was ridiculous.

When he tried to run off with the friars his family even kidnapped him and locked him up—rather like Squire Weston did with Sophie. But in the end, like Sophie, he had his way and went to do his studies amongst the friars—partly at Cologne under Albert the Great, another biologist and also excited by Aristotle. When he had finished there he was sent to Paris, where he instantly became embroiled in the furious infighting caused by the new friars, a sort of 'militant tendency' you might say, trying to infiltrate the rather conservative academic establishment. It didn't help that they came partially equipped, it seemed, with a lot of pagan (Averroistic) Aristotelian views. It helped even less that they were also seen as papal agents trying to subvert the academic independence of the university. Finally the faculty went on strike but by papal pressure Thomas was introduced into the chair of theology, essentially as a strike-breaker I'm afraid.

From then on he spent his life in teaching but also doing various political jobs and was concerned both with the ecumenical movement of the day—reconciliation with the Eastern churches—and with the intellectual and pastoral strategy to be used against the threat of Islam.

In the 1260s when Aquinas was in his forties and at the peak of his form he did a stupendous amount of work, writing commentaries on Aristotle and writing most of the *Summa Theologiae* as well as biblical commentaries. He worked himself literally to death. He had a nervous breakdown and a complete writing block in 1274 and died a few months later. After his death some of his work was condemned by the Church in Paris and in Oxford and nobody was allowed to read him except with a specially written commentary explaining it all away. In fact for half a century almost nobody did read him except his own brethren. Then, as is the way of it, he was rehabilitated and recognized as one of the great masters of medieval thinking. He was also canonized. At the first session of the Council of Trent, which was dominated by Dominicans, it is said that the *Summa* was placed on the altar beside the Bible. I don't know whether this is true but it would certainly have shocked St Thomas very much.

Then nobody read him again for a long time because the Renaissance had happened and European thinking began to be based on that other devout Catholic, René Descartes; there was rationalism on the Continent and empiricism in Britain, which culminated in the liberal bourgeois Enlightenment, and excellent as this was in many ways none of it had much in common with the Aristotelian tradition. Then the intensely conservative Roman Church of the nineteenth century, terrified by the Enlightenment, went back and dug up St Thomas because they thought he might provide the intellectual framework they needed to hold the crumbling fabric of Christianity together. They invented 'Thomism', a specially conservative version of his thought insufficiently liberated from Cartesian questions, and it turned out to be a weapon that twisted in their hands. For it led to a new critical historical study of Aquinas. The new study of the text of Thomas proved if anything more corrosive of the Catholic establishment than even the Enlightenment had been. It was corrosive from inside. Thomas, it emerged, took the Fathers of the Church seriously and took scripture seriously and had a disturbing view of the Church and the sacraments that had been forgotten for centuries or dismissed as Protestant. This development, in the hands especially of the French post-war Dominicans, the new Jesuits, and the Benedictine liturgical revivalists, was the major intellectual power in producing Vatican II in the 1960s, which, amongst other things, put paid to what had been 'Thomism'.

So I suppose we are back again now to a familiar situation in which it is mainly, though not of course exclusively, his brethren who read Thomas. They have in recent years been joined by a quite new crowd, the secular philosophers who have been rediscovering Aristotle and the whole tradition and once again finding it more exciting than anything hitherto available in Europe; they find Aquinas's approach very congenial indeed. They have also been joined by quite a crowd of non-Roman Christians. I noticed that in a recent dictionary of Christian theology there are more references in the index to Thomas Aquinas than to anyone else except Jesus; he easily beats both Paul and Luther.

Chapter 2

Living Things

Life, says Thomas Aquinas in his commentary on Aristotle's book on life, the *De Anima*, is essentially that by which anything has power to move *itself*—taking 'movement' in its wide sense. 'Life' is a word used in several different senses, but related ones. It does not mean the same thing to say that a buttercup is alive and that a tiger is alive, but it is not by a mere accident of the English language, or a pun, that we use the same word 'alive' in both cases. 'Alive' is used, as Aquinas would say, analogically, just as 'love' is used analogically in 'I love a good rare steak' and 'I love my country'. In every case, though, at whatever level we are using the word 'life', we are speaking of what at some level has the power to move *itself*, not just to be at the mercy of others. In this tradition living things are *auto-mobiles*, self-movers. And in this tradition having an *anima* or 'soul' (a term which is also, of course, used analogically) means being, at some level, able to move oneself. All auto-mobiles, at whatever level, have souls—at some level of the word 'soul'. So, in this way of talking, potatoes and cockroaches have souls.

This does not mean—as I think it would mean for, say, Teilhard de Chardin—that potatoes and cockroaches have an elementary form of consciousness or an elementary form of what evolved into human consciousness. (I say I *think* this is what he meant because I find that grasping what Teilhard meant is often a matter of guesswork.) To say, in the

7

traditional manner, that cockroaches have souls is not to say that they have feelings rather like us or that they have 'animal rights'. It is just to say that they are living things, unlike, say, lumps of lead or tape recorders. Cockroaches are self-moving in a sense that tape recorders are not. They are not self-moving in the sense that *I* am, for in my case self-moving has reached the very high level of freedom and creativity, of being responsible for my actions and character; but they are self-moving all the same. So cockroaches are alive, cockroaches have souls, because they are auto-mobiles. It is therefore time we thought about cars.

Most people do not think that cars are alive. Most people draw a sharp distinction between, say, cars and cockroaches. Now is this blind prejudice? Why should *these* auto-mobiles be arbitrarily excluded from the realm of living things? And, while we are on about it, what about computers? Or is it just that we have it wrong; perhaps being alive is *not* to do with being auto-mobile?

Well, me, I come down on the side of saying that cars are not alive because they are not truly auto-mobile. Let us see why.

All living things that are self-moving, at least in the sense of moving physically, must be, as Aristotle pointed out, complex. They have to be made up of parts so that when one part moves another the whole thing moves the whole thing. A leopard is self-moving because the action of one part of it, the brain, which is an action of the leopard, moves another part of it, the legs, which is a movement of the leopard. So it is an action of the leopard (using its brain) that causes a movement of the leopard (using its legs). It is leopard moving leopard—it is self-moving. Now all this depends on both brain and legs being *parts* of the leopard, so that an action of the brain is not just an action of this lump of grey matter but is also an action of the whole leopard; and similarly with the movement of the legs. This implies that if you amputated the leopard's leg, separated it from the whole to which it belongs, it would become a different thing altogether. Before the amputation, if you were so ill-advised as to punch the leopard's leg you would simply be punching the leopard: that is *what it is* you would be punching. After the amputation you would not only not be punching a leopard, you would not even be punching a leg. A detached leg is not a kind of leg, as a dead cow is not a kind of cow or a forged five-pound note is not a kind of five-pound note. And this is not just because we mean by the *word* 'leg' something that is a functioning organ of the animal; it is because in the living beast the leg *is* a functioning organ of the animal. It is because we think this that we think the leopard is self-moving and thus a living thing. It is because we do *not* think that the wheels of a car are, in this sense, *essentially* functioning organs of the car that we do not think that a car is alive. I mean we think of the leopard as the natural unit of which the legs and brain are essentially parts; being a part-of-the-leopard is what it is for the leg to be what it is; it has its existence as what it now is by being a part of the leopard. The whole leopard, so to say, comes first. The parts are secondary. If the leg ceases to be part of the leopard it will turn into something completely different, as mutton is something completely different from a sheep. So a leopard is alive because it has organs which exist as what they are precisely *by* being organs, being functioning parts of a prior whole.

Now the reason why we do not think a car is alive is, I think, because we *assemble* a car from bits which already exist as what they are; and we do not think they turn into something completely different by becoming parts of the car. They are not parts of the car in the sense that legs are part of a leopard. In this case the bits are prior to the car. One striking illustration of this is that while we can dismember a leopard by taking the bits apart, we cannot assemble a leopard simply by adding the bits together. But a car is secondary. It is simply an assemblage of already existing things that have been put in contact with each other. The units in this case are the bits and the car is only a quasi-unit by courtesy of our construction and our culture and our language. It is because *this* is what we think about cars that we think they are not alive. If you belonged to a primitive and blessed community that had no cars, and thus you knew nothing about how cars are assembled from bits, and if you came across one for the first time you would almost certainly think it was alive (as dogs, perhaps, think cars are alive as they go chasing after them). When you learnt more about it you would realize that it was not. What you would learn is that the car is not really a natural unit but only a quasi-unit so that you cannot say literally that the wheels are *organs* of the car. They just act *as though* they were organs of the car; the car is an imitation animal with imitation organs. It is just because the engine is not literally an organ that the action of the engine is not literally an action of the *whole car*, so that when the engine moves the wheels it is not literally the whole car moving the whole car. It is not literally a case of auto-mobility. It is one thing, the engine, moving other things, the wheels, with which it happens to be in contact. (Of course neither the engine nor the wheels are natural units either: they are themselves quasi-units constructed from more primitive natural substances.)

Now, of course, all this account depends on accepting the idea of 'natural units' as distinct from quasi-units that are assembled from them. But this is the way that we do *in fact* think and talk. We speak as though we were familiar with natural units and we distinguish between them and other things. I don't mean, of course, that we are not, for various reasons, allowed to reclassify the world in ways that cut across its natural units; but all such ways of behaving are parasitic on our normal perceptions and normal ways of talking about things. Nor do I mean that our so-called common-sense way of talking of the world is always a reliable clue to what the natural units are; for, after all, we use language mainly not to explain the world but to change it.

I do not know how to give an account of the way we have come to divide up our experienced world into what John

Locke would have called 'natural kinds' or natural units; it is evidently an extremely important part of the business of living with things and interacting with them in all sorts of ways. It seems to me that the idea that we are completely free to reclassify the objects of experience in just any way at all, or (what is the same thing) to use just any names at all to express what is to be a unit in our world, rests on the idea that we are simply spectators of something that stands over against us called the 'world', and we are at liberty to put just any kind of grid we like between the world and our eyes. In fact we are not just spectators, we are involved with and have to cope with things. And recognizing the natural units is part of coping.

So one of the things we have in mind when we say that cockroaches are natural units and thus alive in the way that cars are not natural units is that cockroaches are, and have been, natural units quite regardless of ourselves. There were cockroaches busy being individual natural units before humankind evolved—and, I am told, they will probably go on after we have blown ourselves to bits. Cars evidently have to be assembled by us; cockroaches do not.

But what about synthetic life? Quite apart from genetic engineering, could we not assemble a car complicated enough to be living? We already have computer-controlled cars which do not need a driver. They can detect roadways and obstacles and cope with other traffic by themselves. It would be a small thing for them to have a mechanism by which they would seek out and collect their own petrol and so on. There seems no reason in principle why such a machine should not be able to collect together the necessary materials and construct exact reproductions of itself, which of course would then set about making reproductions in their turn, just as with DNA molecules. We would then have a machine which could move around, feed itself, and *reproduce* itself. Would we not say that it was alive? I think we quite probably would. We could claim to have synthesized life. But notice that we would only be inclined to say it was alive just to the extent that it does *not* need to be synthesized, to the extent that it has an *ancestry* rather than a manufacturer, to the extent that it *does* reproduce itself independently of us, to the extent that it is no longer an artefact but is self-moving and self-reproducing and lives a life of its own. And this, I think, shows that we were right to contrast being alive and being assembled by others. Even if we did assemble such a machine in the first place, we could regard its successors as *alive* just in so far as they no longer need us and escape from our control. We might, incidentally, expect such a synthesized life which is not produced within the balance of a whole evolutionary system to be a danger to the ecological structure that it intrudes upon. I have even heard it suggested that the AIDS virus was originally just such an artificial life form, an unintended spin-off of genetic engineering. But that may be just science fiction.

In any living thing, then, whether natural or (hypothetically) synthetic, the basic characteristic is that it is not an assemblage of prior parts but rather that its parts are *organs* of it, take their meaning from being parts of it and do not exist as *what they now are* before or after being parts of it.

I have just used the word 'meaning' and this was deliberate. For it is with organic structures that we first encounter meaning or significance, which is a certain kind of relationship of part to whole.

Let me repeat that an organic structure is one in which the whole is prior to the parts, so that we give an account of the parts by reference to the whole and not vice versa. It is the account of the *whole* that is, in Aristotle's phrase, *to ti en einai*, 'what it took for the thing to be' in the first place. When you are confronted by a car, 'what it took for all this to be in the first place' is given by speaking of all the various bits that were assembled. The car itself is only the *configuration* of things that were already established as what they were. When, however, you are confronted by a cockroach, 'what it took for all this to be in the first place' is given by an account of the whole cockroach; to consider any one of the bits in isolation is to look at it in the abstract, in abstraction from the whole to which it belongs.

It is characteristic of organic structures that the parts, the organs, exist at *two levels* and this is expressed by the fact that there are two levels of language at which to speak of them. What I mean is that you can, for example, talk of a leg in abstraction from the whole body; you can consider its muscles and nerves and so on and how they operate. Or again you can talk about the leg as an organ, as having a function in the whole body, as, for example, that by which the animal *walks*. Similarly you can consider the eyeball and what it does and what happens to it in terms of lenses and the retina and electric impulses; or again you can see it as an organ of sight, which is to see the relevance of its operation to the whole body. To say that an animal *sees* with its eyes is to say that what happens in the eye is relevant to, makes a difference to, has significance for, the whole body. The way to tell whether an animal is sighted or not is not to look further into an eyeball; it is to find out whether its total behaviour is any different in the dark from in the light. Seeing is an operation done *with* the eye but it is an operation of the entire body. So the eye has an operation of its own which is itself *also* an operation of the *whole* body. That is what I meant by saying that it exists at two levels and that this is expressed by talking about it at two levels. The eye does not undergo electrochemical changes and *also* do something else which is seeing; its sight just *is* its physiological modification as *meaningful* for the whole animal.

With non-organic structures we can also have two levels of talking about the parts. We can consider the car's engine in terms of its internal combustion, its petrol consumption, and so on, or we can talk about it as what makes the car go, its relevance to the behaviour of the whole machine. But in this case the engine does not *exist* at two levels, we just talk of it *as though* it did, just as we talk of the whole machine *as though* it were a whole, a unit, when in fact it is simply an assemblage of bits. A machine, as I have said, is an imitation animal; and so it is convenient to talk of it in organic, animal terms.

Another way of putting this is to say that in an organic structure any of the organs has both an *operation* and a *meaning* to its operation. The meaning of the operation of the eye or the heart or the leg is the part it plays in the operation of the whole structure—just as the meaning of a word is the part it plays in the structure of the whole language.

When we talk of the operation of the eye with reference to the operation of the whole animal, when we talk of it as seeing, when we talk of it as meaningful for the whole structure, we are talking of it as a *vital* operation, as part of the life of the whole animal. Another way of putting this is to say, as Aquinas often does, that seeing is an operation of the soul. When we talk like that we are in some danger of thinking of the soul as another organ alongside the eye and the hand and so on. This temptation is to be resisted. To say that seeing is an operation of the soul is just to say that it is the operation of the organ, the eye, precisely *as* an organ, that is meaningful for the whole body, for the life of the animal. What happens in the eyeball is meaningful for the animal when because of it the animal does something—it runs away, for example, or pounces, or whatever. All the organs of sense are bits of the body which, when they are affected, make the world meaningful for the animal; because of them the animal responds in appropriate ways to its environment, now recognized as significant for it.

It is because the organs are themselves significant parts of the whole body that what affects them is taken up into the structure of the whole body and is thus meaningful. The photoelectric effects on the retina of the eye are *sensations* because the eye is a functional part of a complex structure.

So a living body, a body with a soul, is one in which not only *events* happen but *meaningful* events. If I shine a red light on a white cat it will turn red or at least pink, the redness will be simply the cat's colour; but if I shine it in its *eyes*, just because its eyes are organs it will be a *sensation*, a factor in making the cat's world significant to it—it will, I expect, respond vitally to the colour. The redness will be in the cat's fur simply naturally, as it would be on any reddish surface; but if the light shines in the eye the redness will be in the cat, as Aquinas would say, 'intentionally', as a factor in the cat's interpretation of its world. In other words, we are here at the beginnings of awareness, of knowledge. The cat is not just reddened, it has a sensation of red, it is aware of redness.

In fact I am not at all sure that a cat would be affected (for all I know they are colour-blind), but the same story can be told with, say, the smell of a mouse. There is a great deal of difference between a cat beginning to smell like a mouse because the mouse has foolishly snuggled up against it, and the smell reaching the nostrils of the cat, which are organs. Then the smell becomes a sensation, part of the pattern of the cat's vital activities and tendencies to action.

Chapter 3

Things and Facts

At this point I want to highlight the fact that for Aquinas the world does not consist of facts but of things concerning which there are facts—not just appearances but things with definite natures and which *have* appearances. I shall be trying to distinguish *definitions* from *descriptions*. *Definitions* identify the things, the natural units of the world, prior to stating any contingent fact about individual examples of such units. *Descriptions* identify units not by their fundamental nature but by their impact on *us*. For most of our practical lives we find such mere descriptive identification quite adequate. It is only when we seek to understand the world that we need to attend to definitions. If we want to argue or disagree about the facts it is important to be agreed about what thing these facts are about—so that we are not at cross purposes. Definitions seek to give an account of what I shall call the basic topics of disagreement, or as Wittgenstein might have put it, the rules of the language games we are playing. Definitions, that is, seek to specify the kinds of things that there are. Previously, I was arguing that to give an account of, for example, what 'living' means we need to notice that living beings are amongst the easiest natural units to identify; now I shall be suggesting that our understanding, our scientific investigation of our world, demands that we seek to identify such units. I shall also be arguing that to say that the world consists not of facts but of things is to say that to predicate the *definition* of a subject (as distinct from *describing* it) is just to say what it takes for that thing to exist and to say nothing more.

I have talked about what I call 'natural units' and I have suggested that if life is about self-movement, as Aquinas thought, a living being has to consist of various parts the operations of which are in each case also operations of the whole organism—so that when the operation of a leopard's brain brings about a movement of the leopard's leg it is the leopard moving the leopard. I contrasted the leopard with a car which, although we call it an automobile, is not literally self-moving because it is not a single organic unit but an assemblage of separate things externally connected to each other.

Clearly this picture only makes sense if there *are* such things as natural units, such as leopards, which are distinct from assemblages such as cars. There have been and still are plenty of philosophers who would deny this. The way we divide up our world into distinct objects is, they would argue, a matter of human convenience. We have names for shoes and ships and sealing wax and cabbages and kings, because these are the things we want or need to think about. We draw the boundaries round these areas as arbitrarily as we draw the political boundaries on a map. The United Kingdom is not a natural unit—at least the Scots don't think so, nor do the Welsh; and some of the Irish have their doubts too. So these philosophers would say that shoes and ships and what not have all an equal right to be treated for our purposes (and there are no other relevant purposes) as units or things. Aquinas, as I think you will realize, would recognize only one of the list as a natural unit and that is the cabbage (and it would have to be a living cabbage in the garden, not a dead deracinated corpse in the kitchen).

Previously, I made an appeal to common sense in suggesting that we all agree that a cow is one unit and not, for example, two; but appeal to common sense is an unreliable move in philosophy. You might even say that it is a major function of philosophy to look with some suspicion on common sense. We need something a little more stringent to make sense, if we can, of the view I was putting forward.

But just before doing that I'd like to draw your attention to what seems to be the consequence of rejecting the Aquinas line. He seeks to give an account of what it is to be alive in terms of the material structure of things and notes a difference in the way the bits of a leopard hang together and the way the bits of a car hang together. From these humble beginnings he hopes to go on to give an account of, for example, consciousness and awareness and even (more tentatively) of language and understanding. He starts with publicly available data and reckons he can give an account of what many people would say 'goes on in my head' privately, secretly, and open to me but concealed from others. Those philosophers who would reject at the outset the very notion of leopards as 'natural units' and machines as artificial units have either to say that there is no difference at all, in principle, between leopards and cars (which sounds implausible), or else to provide some other account of what makes living things different. In a great many cases those who can't take on board either the Aristotelian or the mechanistic view have to take refuge in some such notion as 'consciousness', of which we are directly and immediately aware in our heads so that we don't have to have it explained to us. Such a move is characteristic of what I would call the broad Cartesian tradition. The idea is that what we know best is our own thoughts and what sort of thing they are, and we know what life is because we live it. I would not (and certainly Aquinas would not) deny that we can have secret thoughts and private sensations. What I (and Aquinas) would deny is that we can understand what these are by simply introspecting, contemplating the inside of our heads, so to speak. I say this simply because it often helps to know what a speaker is against as well as what he is for. Descartes thought that our own minds are the thing we know best and are most certain about; getting to know about the material world was much trickier. Aquinas thought the opposite: that the natures of *material* things were what we knew best and it was very difficult to talk about our mental life (and even more difficult to talk about God).

A key word here is 'talk'. Although Aquinas frequently and cheerfully speaks of understanding as, metaphorically, seeing, in fact he thinks of understanding not on the model of a sensation, *sight*, but on the model of an activity, *talking*. You can best understand him by beginning with the idea that solitary thinking is a kind of talking to yourself. This idea would not be quite as ascribable to Aquinas as it would be to a great many Anglo-American philosophers these days, but it is a good approximation to start with. Aquinas certainly says that anything I can think I can express in words but he also has an analysis of understanding in terms of concepts and 'interior words' and so on. In what I shall be going on to say, I shall often try to explain what Thomas is getting at by starting from the linguistic end. This is because I think this is more intelligible and less misleading for people in our present age. The trouble with the alternative way of putting things is that it sounds to us—though it did not, I think, to Aquinas's contemporaries—as though he were describing understanding as the product of some kind of interior mental mechanism, and this would be wholly to miss his point.

Let us begin, then, with some simple indicative sentences and let us think about them in their literal use (as distinct from the metaphorical).

'The cat was extremely hungry' and 'The telephone was extremely hungry'. These are both well-formed sentences in English, unlike, for example, 'Very rarely, undoubtedly frightens curiously yesterday', which sounds like, and is, gibberish—though the flexibility of any language is such that you could probably invent a far-fetched use for it.

'The cat was extremely hungry' is a perfectly sensible *sentence* which could be used in a particular context to make a true or false *statement*. In this sentence 'The cat' is the subject section and its function is to *stand for* or *refer to* what is being talked about. In Aquinas's language it is 'taken materially' (*tenetur materialiter*) and the rest of the sentence, 'was extremely hungry', is the predicate and this does not stand for or refer to anything but has a meaning. It is, in the Aquinas jargon, 'taken formally' (*tenetur formaliter*). This insight, a commonplace among medieval logicians, was lost to sight in the Dark Ages of the Renaissance and had to be rediscovered by Gottlob Frege. The *sentence* itself is not true or false; those adjectives belong to the *statement* (what Aquinas would call the *iudicium* or judgement that may be expressed by such a sentence). We can know the meaning of a sentence without using it to make a statement. For Aquinas, understanding the meaning of a word or a sentence is what he calls the first operation of the intellect (*simplex apprehensio*) whereas grasping truth or being occurs in the second operation of the intellect, *iudicium*, asserting something with the language. 'The cat was extremely hungry' is a well-formed sensible sentence whether or not it is being used to say anything. 'The telephone was extremely hungry' is a well-formed English sentence but is also a piece of nonsense. If you tried to make a statement with it you would not be able to say anything true, but also you would not be able to say anything false in the way in which 'The cat is extremely hungry' might be used to say something false. I think this is because the nonsense sentence cannot be used to make a statement at all. Nonsense sentences, however, unlike gibberish, are valid, and indeed valuable, parts of the language; we use them, for example, to tell fairy-stories and children's tales where trees and animals talk.

So, in summary:

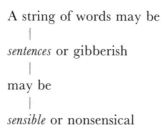

A string of words may be
|
sentences or gibberish
|
may be
|
sensible or nonsensical

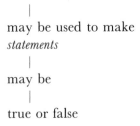

may be used to make
statements

may be

true or false

Now I would like to ask: What skills do we use to make these various distinctions?

We distinguish sentences from gibberish by *grammatical* skills by which we understand how various 'parts of speech' fit together or don't.

We distinguish sensible from nonsensical sentences by *semantic* skills, understanding the *meanings* of the words. We say such things as 'Telephones cannot really be hungry'.

We distinguish true from false statements by living in our world and talking with others in our world, arguing and so on. We could call this 'experience' had not the word been hijacked by empiricists who imagine that experience is simply being hit by sense-data.

The same statement can of course be made by many different sentences. If someone says to me: 'Do you think Kidlington is bigger than London?' and I say 'Yes', I am making the statement that I think Kidlington is bigger than London, but I am not sure whether a grammarian would count 'Yes' as a sentence at all. And, of course, the same statement may be made with sentences in different *languages*: 'J'adore Paris' can be used in French to make the same statement as 'I love Paris' in English.

All this is simply to explain a terminology of sense, nonsense, and statement which is not St Thomas's but my own and partially borrowed from other philosophers.

Let us look a little more closely at how sentences do and do not make sense. This, I have suggested, has to do with the meanings of the terms used. It is because of what 'the cat' means that we can attach to it either the predicate 'is hungry' or 'is not hungry'. Nothing in the meaning of 'the cat' disposes us to favour either predicate but (unlike 'telephone', which forbids both) it allows for either. We have a choice between the two equally sensible sentences. We might say that the meaning of 'the cat', what sort of thing a cat is, authorizes certain contrary pairs of predicates and not others. It was Aristotle who first pointed out the great difference between on the one hand *using* one or other of the authorized predicates 'is hungry' or 'is not hungry' and, on the other hand, talking about what it is that *authorizes* them both: the meaning of the word 'cat' or what sort of thing a cat is. To say *what something is* is not to describe it (as you do when you say it is hungry); it is to *define* it. Definition and description are quite separate uses of language. Definition delimits the area within which descriptive statements (true or false) may be made. Because of our different experiences we may disagree about whether the cat is hungry or, say, merely greedy: let us say we disagree about the facts. But if we do not agree about *what* a cat is we cannot even *disagree* about whether it is hungry or not. To know *what something is* is to have, as it were, a topic for discussion; if we do not have the same idea of what we are talking about we shall simply be at cross purposes.

I remember being scandalized when I first read Aquinas saying that the first thing we understand is *what* something is, or its essence. Since he also said that the senses do not tell us the essences of things and that human knowledge originates in sense experience, and since, moreover, Aquinas is famous for having said that we do not know the essence of even a housefly, there seemed to be some terrible muddle here.

What we need to keep before our minds is that for Aquinas, the model for understanding is talking. In this he stands in vivid contrast to, say, David Hume, who in the superbly provocative opening of his *Treatise of Human Nature* says this:

All the perceptions of the human mind resolve themselves into two distinct kinds, which I shall call IMPRES-

SIONS and IDEAS. The difference betwixt these consists in the degrees of force and liveliness, with which they strike upon the mind, and make their way into our thought or consciousness. Those perceptions, which enter with most force and violence, we may name *impressions*; and under this name I comprehend all our sensations ... By *ideas* I mean the faint images of these in thinking and reasoning ... I believe it will not be very necessary to employ many words in explaining this distinction. Every one of himself will readily perceive the difference betwixt feeling and thinking.[1]

Everyone will indeed perceive this difference; the question is whether she will recognize it as like the difference between hearing a shout and hearing a whisper (as Hume here suggests) or whether it is like the difference between, say, the passivity of *feeling* the cold and the activity of *saying* to ourselves or others 'It's a cold day', which is what Aristotle and Aquinas would say.

But back to the housefly. Of course Aquinas knew what a housefly was. What he meant was that so far nobody had come to an understanding of what precisely it takes for something to be a housefly, which would be to know what a housefly is scientifically. Since then, I imagine, we have got a great deal nearer to this aim: we are approaching the goal of giving an accurate definition of the beast. But what Aquinas (who thought that human knowledge consists in the answering of asked questions) is saying is that if we ask a question about houseflies we will get nowhere if someone answers under the impression we are talking about televisions or how the Jamaicans would curry a goat. We start, in other words, with a rough idea of what a housefly is that we can agree about, and then we can, if we want to, after a lot of hard work, approach a more scientific account of the essence of houseflyness.

---

[1] David Hume, *A Treatise of Human Nature*, ed. L. A. Selby-Bigge, 2nd edn (Oxford: Clarendon Press, 1978), pp. 1–2.

Aristotle invented the idea of the *categories*, which are not a classification of *things* but of predicates: and not a grammatical classification of the predicates of sentences but a classification of what we are predicating of things by means of sentences when we use them to make *statements*. To make this point, that the categories are categories of predicates not of things, Aquinas prefers to call them the *praedicamenta*. Whenever we seek to say what sort of thing this is, for Aquinas we are in the business not of *describing* it but of *defining* its nature, and our statement is in the category (or *praedicamentum*) of substance. And I am suggesting that this means indicating how we should subsequently talk about it, how we should disagree about it perhaps. We are defining the range of contingent, accidental predicates that may sensibly be asserted or denied of it. If people ask us 'What colour is an electron?' or 'How heavy is the equator?' we know that they do not understand *what* an electron or the equator is. We are at cross purposes.

If someone says, 'Absolutely the only thing I know about some particular plig is that this one happens to be avaricious,' he is mistaken. If it really is avaricious then he also knows, without adverting to it, that the plig is a kind of thing that *can* be either avaricious or not, and this narrows down the range of things it might be. It cannot, for example, be like a rainbow or a date-palm, neither of which can be, or even fail to be, avaricious. To be avaricious implies (in an odd sense of 'implies') that it is a certain kind of thing and not another. Perhaps it would be better to say that it *presupposes* rather than implies that it is a certain (very vaguely defined) sort of thing.

Moreover if it is *true* that some plig is avaricious we also know (again not because it is *stated* but because it is *presupposed*) that at least one plig *exists*, for being avaricious has to be something-being-avaricious. Being avaricious is what Aquinas calls an accidental predicate. There cannot be avarice unless there is some man, woman, or child (or maybe some other being) who is avaricious. Avarice cannot just stand by itself; it has to be the avarice *of* (or *in*) some subject. As Aquinas says neatly in Latin, an accident like avarice is not so much *est* as *inest*.

When we make a *statement* in the category of substance we are saying purely and simply *what* is and refraining from expressing any other opinion about it, but we are delimiting what range of additional things may be said about it truly or falsely—what accidental features it may have or lack.

In modern English we use the word 'definition' with respect to the meanings of words. But *definitio* for Aquinas, and for Aristotelians in general, applies to natures or essences. Natures are not just the meanings of words (as nominalists would say) nor are they existing objects (as Platonists would say); they are the essences of existing things. So horseness is that by which something is a horse; and it is by having horseness that it exists. For Aquinas (unlike Plato), there can be no essence which is not that of an existing thing; and amongst creatures there can be no existing thing without a distinct and definite essence. Essence or nature is that by which a thing exists: a thing exists by having an essence. Aquinas says that if there is nothing in existence that has the nature expressed by a particular definition, then what looks like a definition, an account of an essence, is simply an explanation of the meaning of a word. In ordinary language we have very few words whose meaning is simply *what* something is, words which simply signify an essence; they are nearly always, as it were, adulterated by some additional accidental information. And this is for the very good reason that we name things not in order to celebrate their essential nature but to indicate our interest in them. When I say that Arkle was a racehorse I am not simply saying *what* Arkle was; for a racehorse is a horse that is apt or fit or used for racing, but what-Arkle-was was a *horse*, and when he was injured and no longer apt or fit or used for racing he remained the same horse. It was only when he had to be put down that he ceased to be *what he was* and became something quite other, a collection of chemicals that we call the corpse of a horse. We can say that Arkle's essential nature, the sort of thing he was,

was to be a horse and it was only when he lost *this* that he
ceased to be what he was and simply speaking ceased to be.
When he stopped racing he lost an accidental being. When he
stopped being a horse he stopped existing altogether.

Another way of putting this is to say that when we make a
statement in the category of substance about something,
saying what sort of thing it is, we are saying what it takes for
that thing simply to exist. Again, Aristotle's phrase is *to ti en
einai*: what it was for Arkle to be in the first place quite apart
from what colour he was or whether he was engaged in racing,
or whether he was in Dublin or Cheltenham or Paris. Yet
another way of putting this is to say that being a horse is being
a *natural unit* whereas being a racehorse is not. Aquinas's
phrase for a natural unit is an *ens per se* (a being as such); thus
a horse exists by being as such, by being a horse, whereas a
racehorse does not exist by being a racehorse, just because he
may stop racing and yet still exist by being a horse.
Nevertheless we quite rightly, for practical purposes of daily
life, treat a racehorse as a unit, just as we treat a car as a unit.
Aquinas would call such a quasi-unit an *ens per accidens* or *ens
secundum accidens*. We treat a racehorse or a car or a table as
though it were a natural unit, as though a car existed by being
a car even though a car is in fact an assemblage of units each
of which exists by being what it separately is. And we do this
for our own convenience. We are interested in cars for getting
about in, for enjoying ourselves, for polluting the atmosphere
and so on. It is only the scientific observer who looks at cars
for their *own* sake and not for ours, and so analyses the car into
its natural component parts. A car or a racehorse is only a
quasi-being because of the accidental circumstance of being
treated as one thing by *us* and in our language (an *ens per
accidens*). A car, as I have said, is an imitation animal and it is,
therefore, an imitation natural unit, a quasi-natural unit by
courtesy of our interests and our imposition of names. It is just
such a collection of beings, treated by us as a unit, that
Aquinas calls an *ens per accidens*. Other examples are an

27

audience, or a constellation of stars in the sky, or an exhibition of pictures, or a postman.

Note, in conclusion, that an *ens per accidens* is not the same as an accidental being. Blueness is an accident, as is being tall or being in Oxford or being able to speak French. These are all accidents because they are incidental to some substance, they *inest* in a subject rather than simply *est* of themselves. The combination of a substance and an accident, if we have a name for it, is an *ens per accidens*—as with a postman, who is a combination of being a human being (substance) and being employed to deliver letters (an accident).

Chapter 4

Sensation, Language, and Individuals

At the end of Chapter 2 I said: 'There is a great deal of difference between a cat beginning to smell like a mouse because the mouse has foolishly snuggled up against it, and the smell reaching the nostrils of the cat, which are organs. Then the smell becomes a sensation, part of the pattern of the cat's vital activities and tendencies to action.' Now I want to move forward with this thought in mind.

If you have a magnetic needle it will *tend* to point to magnetic north; it will do so unless prevented. This is because of a characteristic the magnetic needle has, a certain alignment of some of its molecules. Now it belongs to animals such as cats that they can have tendencies not only because of characteristics that they naturally have (like falling if you let go of them because they are naturally heavier than air) but also because of characteristics that they have 'intentionally', sensations that they receive. So the cat will have a tendency to pounce because it *smells* a mouse (because it has the smell of the mouse 'intentionally') or because it *sees* or *hears* its movements (because it has the appearance of the mouse intentionally). In this case the movement of the cat is mediated by sensations, by awareness, by the cat having a sensuous interpretation of its world. It moves because of what the world *means* to it. To say this is to suggest that talk of a stimulus 'triggering' the response of the cat is misleading because it oversimplifies the situation. The metaphor of the pressure on the trigger making the gun fire won't do, because the effect of the stimulus to the cat is to produce not a movement but a *tendency* to move. The stimulus enters into a whole pattern of other stimuli. The tendency it produces becomes part of a balance of other stimuli and the outcome is therefore nothing like as predictable as would be the case with a trigger and an explosion. Pavlovian experiments to make dogs predictably salivate, or whatever, work by artificially placing the animal in conditions in which other responses are ruled out. This artificial limitation is, of course, the correct procedure if you are, for example, investigating the effect of introducing an extra methyl radical into an organic molecule, or the precise effect of decreased moisture on the biological ageing of a plant. Your experimental aim is to eliminate other processes and reactions and look at this particular one in isolation. And if you look at animal behaviour with these same techniques it is not surprising if you get results which suggest that the animal is nothing other than a machine. The experiment is, so to say, rigged to treat it as a machine. The animal's *not* being a machine is nothing other than the fact that its whole experience, the very many complex stimuli it is receiving, ought to be taken into account together if you want to give a correct account of it. The animal is a whole which is prior to its parts and to treat its parts in isolation (though illuminating for many purposes) is to abstract from the full truth about the animal.

To say, then, that the cat 'has a soul' or 'has life' is not to say that there is an extra invisible organ or an 'entelechy' that the Pavlovian or behaviourist has overlooked. It is not to add to the description of the cat; it is to say *what sort of descriptions* are appropriate to it; it is to say what sort of being a cat is; it is to say 'what it took for it to be a cat' (*to ti en einai*) in the first place. It is to say which investigative techniques are appropriate to it and which are merely dealing with abstractions from the total reality.

If you decide that a cat is such a living animal (and this does seem the common-sense thing to decide) then you can make sense of saying that the cat has experiences, sensations, and moreover that it has memory and can learn, that it can do things willingly or unwillingly, that it can suffer and search and try to do things and recognize itself over against its world. None of these things can literally be said of machines; and none of these things necessarily entails having what people call a human consciousness.

I shall now be suggesting that the specifically human kind of life, or soul, involves not simply expressing its sensations and perceptions *as tendencies to act* or behave within a complex set of such tendencies but also expressing them by means of symbols or language. They do not just have (as monkeys have and typewriters do not) a lifetime but also a life story. This, as I hope to convince you, makes the human animal more animal than others. If by being animate or animated or having a soul, we mean acting as a whole and not simply as a set of smaller things that are in contact with each other (as with a machine), and thus to be in a certain way self-moving, auto-mobile, in possession of itself, then the capacity to symbolize our world, to express our experience linguistically, is to make us even more in charge of our behaviour and of ourselves.

So to have a linguistic (or what Aquinas calls a *rational*) life is to be more animate, more alive, more of an animal, than brute beasts. Understanding, says Aquinas, is a form of life and indeed is the most perfect that there is in life. For Aquinas there is a kind of continuum between the lower kinds of life, the plants, which have certain vital processes such as metabolism and growth (in a very primitive way they make the world their own; they have 'their world'), on through the animals which interpret the world sensually and behave in this way or that because of their sensual interpretation, on up to the rational, linguistic animals, which also interpret the world through symbols that they have themselves created. The idea that the intellectual life is simply to be contrasted with and set over

31

against the sensual life is quite foreign to Aquinas. Rationality, for him, transcends sensation but is in a way continuous with it.

Non-linguistic animals interpret their world through what he calls the *species sensibilis*, which is formed in sensation. The *species sensibilis* is the sensation (in the nose or the ear or the eye) as relevant to the rest of the animal body and its behaviour. When the cat looks at the king the appearance which is in the king as a set of physical properties (*naturaliter*) is (given suitable illumination) in the cat's eye as part of the cat's life, as making a difference to what it will do next (*intentionaliter*).

An explanatory word here, perhaps, about *intentio*. This, for St Thomas, is taken in its most general sense as a *tending towards* something. We speak of an action being intentional, or done with a certain intention, when we mean it is aimed at achieving some end or purpose; it tends towards that end. Now the appearance of the king in the king is simply there as a set of chemical and physical facts, and when that appearance is in the eye of the cat, we can, of course, see this also as a set of chemical and physical facts about the eye. But what makes it a sensation is just that it is in the eye as tending towards something, as sensually interpreting a bit of the world, as inviting some kind of behaviour on the part of the cat in view of this interpretation. In a fairly parallel way Aquinas sees the meaning in a word not as a set of physical properties of the word but as the word's function in interpreting some nature or other, as signifying the pattern of the world. Human nature is in *people* as what they *have* in order to be what they *are*; human nature is in my *mind* or in the phrase 'human nature' as an interpretative account of what people are.

I want to go on talking about language and thought but first it may be helpful to look at the individual animal as member of a species.

Just as each part of an animal is an organ, a functioning part of the whole body, so there is a sense in which each individual animal is itself a kind of organ, a functioning part of its species. First of all let us be clear that when we speak of an animal species we are not speaking of some kind of logical classification. The species *dog* is not the class of all animals which resemble each other in certain respects. The species is an historical material entity. By the species to which a dog belongs I mean its ancestry and its progeny. There is a physical and not just a conceptual connection between all dogs; they are genetically and not merely logically related.

I shall be comparing and contrasting the way that an individual animal belongs to, is part of, a species, its *genetic* community, and the way that the human animal belongs also to a culture, its *linguistic* community. I shall be suggesting that to have symbols and words is to have a particular way of belonging to a community, rather as to have genes is to have another way of belonging to a community.

I say that an individual dog is in a sense an *organ* of the dog species because there is a sense in which just as the whole animal is prior to its parts, so the species is prior to the individual and the individual can most properly be understood as a part of the species. A dog has to be born of other members of the species and much of its behaviour is intelligible only as a functioning part of this species, as that by which the species is perpetuated.

Animals arrive equipped genetically with a whole lot of behavioural tendencies; they do not have to learn to take flight or to attack in the face of certain dangers; they do not have to learn to be sexually attracted to each other or to make preparations for rearing their young. All these tendencies are genetically supplied, supplied by the species; and if they were not, the species would not survive. Just as we can see teeth and claws as organs by which the individual survives, so we might see the individual as a kind of organ by which the tradition of the genes survives. This explains what is sometimes called the 'altruistic' behaviour of animals. In the defence of their young they may sacrifice their own lives, transcending their individual self-preservation for the sake of *species* preservation. They will be unable not to.

The genetic determinants of animal behaviour, of course, change with changes in their environment, but only by the cumbersome mechanism of natural selection. The cultural demands upon the linguistic animal change with enormously greater rapidity. *We* have history instead of evolution, and we have the handing on of acquired characteristics that we call *tradition*. In the evolutionary process the slightest variation requires a generation; we can change culturally within our lifetimes—every time we are convinced by an argument or converted to a new way of life or conduct or endure a revolution of any kind. All this comes about by the use of symbols and the systems of symbols that we can broadly call language. It is because of language that we are alive in a different way from other animals and it is because of language that we are self-transcendent in a different way from other animals.

Let us take a look at symbols. We saw previously that there is a difference between shining a red light on the white fur of a cat and shining it in its eyes, simply because the eyes are a particular kind of organ. In the one case the redness is in the cat as a pink colour of its surface, in the other it is present as a sensation, as part of the cat's interpretation of its world. What this presence amounts to is that the sensation *plays a part in the cat's response to its world, its tendency to behave*. The sensation occurs *in the cat* as a perceived *meaning* that affects its behaviour.

Let us then think of a sheep's recognition of a chunk of its environment—say a wolf—as dangerous and to be avoided. This is, of course, the combination of a great many present sensations, memories, and instincts.

The dangerousness of the wolf exists in one way in the wolf (it *is*, as a matter of fact, dangerous to sheep) and in another way in the sense structures of the sheep (it is *perceived* as dangerous, or the danger exists as a meaning in the sheep). When the dangerousness of the wolf impinges on the sheep, the sheep does not become dangerous. The dangerousness is present in the sheep intentionally and this amounts to certain behavioural tendencies like running away.

The sheep is acting as though this chunk of its environment had a certain meaning for it, a significance for its own life. The dangerousness which in the wolf is a mere natural characteristic of it becomes in the nervous system of the sheep a meaning; a motive, for example, for action. We rightly say: the sheep ran away *because* it perceived the wolf and perceived it as dangerous.

Now what I want to stress here is that it is the same dangerousness, what Aristotle or Aquinas would call the same 'form', or pattern of meaning (more of that in a moment), that is present in one way in the wolf itself and in another way in the nervous system and brain of the sheep. In the former case it is present as the pattern of what the wolf *is in fact* like. In the latter case it is present as a pattern *playing its part* in the structure of the sheep's vital behaviour. It is the *same* form, that is, if the sheep is in a healthy state, in a state to survive, if it is seeing the world normally. There might be a confused, mad sheep which saw (interpreted) grass as dangerous and wolves as edible; but it would not live long. Ordinarily it is the *same* form that is objectively or 'naturally' in the thing perceived and intentionally in the perceiver, as a perception, as an evaluation or interpretation of its world. So it is the same form that could be an account of what is the case in the material wolf and also an account of what is going on in the material nervous system of the sheep. In the nervous system it exists as a *meaning*, as *part* of a structure as relating to *other* parts of the structure; what happens in the sheep's eyes and nose is relevant to what it does with its feet. Notice that the dangerousness which was a simple physical *fact* in the wolf has now become in the sheep a matter of the *relevance* of what is happening in one organ to the behaviour of the whole organism. The dangerousness *in the wolf* is made of bone and tooth and muscle; as a perception it is made of *relevance*. The perception is not itself a physical object; it is the relation of one physical object to others. It exists at a certain level of abstraction. Aquinas does not hesitate to say that the perceptions of brute animals are 'spiritual', meaning that an animal acts in terms of such relations of relevance and not simply as, say, a billiard ball is pushed physically by another. 'Spiritual', then, because belonging to the first move in transcending matter.

I think it is now time we thought a bit about matter and form—though these modern words do not quite capture what Aquinas meant by *materia* and *forma*. Never mind; they are the nearest thing we have. 'Matter' and 'form' are terms devised to solve problems about two pervasive truths about the natural world: that there are individual things, and that they change. I'll talk about change briefly later; for now, let's have a look at individuals.

Let us consider Fido and Rover, two dogs. We can say 'Fido is a dog' and 'Rover is a dog' and in each case we may suppose that we are giving some kind of account of *what* each of them is. To say 'Fido is a dog' is to give an account of his nature; it is to say what he is and to say nothing else about him. It is not to say where he is or what colour he is. It says simply what it takes for him to be at all, and, if the sentence is being used to make a true statement, it asserts that Fido *exists*, and nothing more. Such statements are, if you remember, statements in the category of substance; they tell you the substance (nature) of Fido and Rover but not any accidental facts about them— which would be asserted by statements in one of the other categories (quantity, quality, or whatever).

Now if Fido is a dog and Rover is a dog and 'is a dog' is the same predicate with the same meaning in both cases, then why is Fido not Rover? Why are they distinct individuals although what it takes for them to exist is the same in each? One beguiling answer is to say: 'That's easy: they are both dogs, but one is the dog in the garden and the other is the dog in the kitchen; or one is brown and the other is black.' Unfortunately, however, this will not do. For to say '*One* is the dog in the garden and the *other* is the dog in the kitchen' is to presuppose that we already understand, can give an account of 'the one . . . and the other', which is the very thing we are supposed to be giving an explanation of. If you ask 'How come I can talk about one dog and another dog?,' it is not helpful to say, 'Well, you see, one is black and the other is brown.' You could generalize this and say: 'No accidental predicate, like being in the garden or being black, is going to provide an account of what it is for Fido to be this individual dog and not that individual dog.'

The problem does not arise, of course, with Fido and my cat Clementina, for what it takes for Clementina to exist is being a *cat* and what it takes for Fido to exist is being a *dog*, and this is a clear distinction between them. Even if they are both black and both in the garden, this has no tendency to imply that they are identically the same thing.

There have been, and probably still are, philosophers who have not agreed about this (or have not seen this point)— Leibniz, for one, and also (in one of his phases) Bertrand Russell. They have thought that if X is not identical with Y then there must be something that can be predicated of X and not of Y.

Conventionally in the twentieth century this problem has been discussed by asking: what do we mean when we announce the relatively recent astronomical discovery that 'The morning star is the evening star'? The morning star is the last bright light to remain in the sky after dawn and the evening star is the first one to appear in the evening. The discovery is that in the first place it is not a star at all but a planet, and in the second place they are both the *same* planet, Venus.

Aquinas's answer is to remind us of what he thinks about the difference between how words function in the subject part of a sentence and in the predicate part. For him words in the subject place are there essentially to name, to pick out what it is you are talking about. His phrase is *tenetur materialiter*—as we should say, 'are names used to refer to something'. They have meaning as well, of course (for Aquinas, all words, even proper names, have meaning quite apart from which thing they are naming or refer to), but their essential job in the subject place is to indicate the subject, the thing talked about. Words in the predicate, by contrast, are not names and do not refer, but only have meaning; they *tenetur formaliter*.

Take 'The man next door | is not a plumber.' Who is not a plumber? Why, the man next door; this is the chap referred to, named, by the subject phrase. Contrast this with the predicate words. It would be merely foolish to ask 'Which plumber isn't he?' because words in the predicate place are not there to be a name; they are there for their meaning, not for their reference. Aquinas, however, notes an *exception* to this which he calls a *predicatio per identitatem*—or, as we should say, an identity statement. He says that this is not properly a predication, because the words that seem to be in the predicate place are not used for the sake of their meaning but, like the ones in the subject place, as names to refer. In other words both the subject and the predicate are now names. He would say that 'The morning star is the evening star' means 'What is named by "The morning star" is what is named by "The evening star".'

Now it is precisely this that Wittgenstein rediscovered in the *Tractatus Logico-Philosophicus*:

> $a = b$ means then, that the sign 'a' is replaceable by the sign 'b'

and

> Identity of the object I express by identity of the sign and not by means of a sign of identity.[1]

---

[1] Ludwig Wittgenstein, *Tractatus Logico-Philosophicus*, tr. C. K. Ogden (London: Routledge and Kegan Paul, 1922), 4.241, 5.53.

What both Aquinas and Wittgenstein are saying is that identity or non-identity, whether Fido and Rover are identical or not, is not a matter of *what you say* about them but of what it is you are talking *about*. It is not a matter, as Leibniz and Russell thought, of whether what you *say about* Fido is the same as what you *say about* Rover, but whether what you say about Fido is also about Rover.

So, for Aquinas and Wittgenstein what makes it the case that Fido and Rover are distinct individuals of the same nature is not anything at all that can be said about them or understood about them but simply that we pick them out separately. 'This is one and that is the other' is not to describe either of them, not to attribute to either of them any meaningful feature, not to predicate anything of them. 'One' and 'other' do not function that way: they are words that accompany some kind of bodily behaviour, they belong to the job of pointing out.

What we have in mind, for Aquinas, are concepts of natures or meanings. To have such concepts is to be able to handle words or other symbols. The meaning of a word, the concept we have in mind, is never for Aquinas an individual thing but always a nature; the meaning of the word 'dog' is a nature common to countless individuals—it is, as the medievals said, a 'universal'. Wittgenstein makes the same point when he shows, in the *Philosophical Investigations*, that there is no such thing as 'ostensive definition'—that is to say, you cannot teach anyone the meaning of, say, the word 'giraffe' *simply* by pointing at a giraffe. How is he to know what you are pointing at? Its neck? Its colour? Its height? Indeed, how is he to know what pointing is, and which direction to look?

So, for Aquinas, to know about, to try to understand, an individual we need more than a mind, we need a body and its sensual awareness. If we had no bodies we might know a great deal of rather beautiful theoretical physics but it would be indistinguishable from pure mathematics, we would not be able to lay hold on what it was about. Put it another way. The only way to be quite sure a cat is the same cat is to keep your eye on it; it is a matter not of your mind but of your bodily senses.

So being a cat, being an individual cat, is not just having the cat-nature (plus as many accidental features as you like); it is also being this cat and not that, where 'this' and 'that' are not additional bits of description but the music that accompanies the bodily dance that we call 'pointing'.

Cats always are individual cats; 'catness' is just the meaning of the word 'cat', a particular structure of being which is to be found in nature and which differs in intelligible ways from dogness and giraffeness. But catness itself does not exist as an item in nature. Catness is, if you like, the intelligibility of the cat, but no cat is just its intelligibility. There is also the fact of its being this cat and not that one. And even if it were the last cat in the world, which God forbid, it would still be just this cat and not another because there might be others, and used to be others. So any individual thing (and the world with which we are engaged through our senses is nothing but individual things) is constituted by a factor of intelligibility, by which it can be taken up into minds as the meaning of words, and also a factor of unintelligibility, a surd which we can only grasp bodily, sensibly. This complexity of individual things is what Aquinas is talking about when he speaks of their form (the intelligible factor) and their matter, their individuation.

Chapter 5

Change, Language, Reasons, and Action

I was speaking at the end of the previous chapter about matter and form; and I said that these terms were devised for use in giving an account of two pervasive features of our world: that there are many individuals of the same nature or species and that these individuals change. I talked about how what accounts for individuation is the unintelligible sensible materiality of things. That is to say, it is by our bodily senses that we pick out individuals even though to our minds, which are capacities for deploying meanings, two individuals may be exactly the same. Now I want to talk about change.

An Aristotelian, like Aquinas, recognizes broadly two sorts of change. There is the alteration of something in respect of one of its accidental features—as when the dog which has been in the garden comes into the kitchen. One accidental feature has been replaced by another but it is the same dog; it is *substantially*, as to its nature, its substance, the same. Parmenides, who thought that things were exactly what they actually are and that therefore the dog-in-the-garden could not possibly become the dog-not-in-the-garden but in the kitchen, denied that such change was possible. For him things were like numbers: 6 just is 6, and if you add, say, 1 to it, it ceases to be 6 and is replaced by 7. (7 is not 6 with an accidental extra 1. It is a distinct new number.) Against this

Aristotle argued that a proper account of what Fido is does not simply stop short at what he actually is at any given moment but must allow for what he could be, what he is potentially. He is actually in the garden (this is an accidental form that he has), but he has the potential to be not in the garden but in the kitchen. This potentiality does not mean *power*. We are not saying that the seeds of being in the kitchen are within Fido or that he will grow into a kitchen-dweller. We simply mean he has a passive capacity to have this happen to him and still remain the dog he is.

The second sort of change that an Aristotelian recognizes is the more radical one in which Fido does not simply lose an accidental form and acquire another while remaining Fido, remaining this dog. In this more radical change Fido loses the very substantial form by which he is a dog and by which he exists at all. It is by a form that anything is actual. *Forma dat esse*, says Aquinas: form gives existence. It is by a form that anything is. Fido *is in the garden* by an accidental form; Fido *is*, simply speaking, by the substantial form of a dog. Aquinas has a special name for the substantial form of a living thing, such as Fido; he calls it his *anima*, his life or his soul. When Fido loses his soul, his life, he ceases to exist by turning into something else, into another substance—or, in this case, a number of other substances, for the corpse of a dog is not a single natural unit but a heap of chemicals. (We must remember, of course, that this whole talk of 'natural units' was rejected by 'atomists', such as Epicurus (*c*. 300 BC) and Lucretius (*c*. 50 BC), who saw all change as an accidental change of arrangement amongst imperishable *atoms*. For them nothing ever comes into existence or perishes.)

In the case of accidental change—coming into the kitchen— there is change of what is incidental but a continuity of substance. It is still Fido who is in the kitchen; his substantial form remains. It is the same actual substance that first has these accidents and then those. When Fido dies there is no such continuing substance common to the living and the dead Fido.

There is nevertheless a kind of continuity, for we say 'This is the corpse *of* Fido.' We mean that this corpse was made out of Fido, who is no longer here. There is nothing actual of Fido here. However, since Fido perished there was in him the possibility of perishing, and this is what Aquinas calls *materia prima* ('prime matter'). *Materia prima*, he is quite clear, is nothing actual; it is the perishability of actual material things. It is a passive openness to new actuality, new forms. It is the potentiality which will be actualized by new form to be a new thing. For Aquinas potentiality can only occur in what is actual: 'Act is prior to potency.' He has no use for sheer vacant possibility. It is always the possibility *of* some existing thing. The notion, popular these days, of 'possible worlds' would make no sense to him. There cannot be possibility except *in* a universe. So-called 'logical possibility' refers to possible well-formed sentences in a language. Prior to creation there was no potential universe waiting to be actualized by form. Our universe was not possible before it was created.

So the potentiality to be actualized by the later substantial forms which give actuality to the chemicals that compose Fido's corpse *is* the potentiality in Fido to perish. We might say misleadingly that what is common to Fido and the corpse is *materia prima*, which was first in Fido actualized by the form of a dog and then in the corpse actualized by new forms; having the same *materia prima* constitutes the continuity. But this would be dangerously misleading because it verges on hypostasizing *materia prima*. Things can only be the same by having the same form (you have to be the same *dog* or the same *shade of blue* or the same piece of *paper*; you cannot be just the same). If you want to attach a meaning to 'same matter' you will, as usual, have to resort to your own body. No account of the collection of substances which is Fido's corpse will tell you that it is the corpse of Fido. For a while, of course, there will be circumstantial hints. It will look a bit like Fido for a while before it begins to fall to pieces. The only way to be sure this is the corpse of Fido is to be bodily present at his deathbed and see him die. You have to keep your eye on him. And this possibility of sensually verifying that the corpse was made out of Fido is what Aquinas means by saying that the corpse has the *same 'materia prima'* as Fido.

Now let us get back to animals and especially human animals.

It is part of what we mean when we say that this is an *animal* that it is *alive* (unlike a car), that it is an *organism*, and that its behaviour is to be spoken of in terms of perceiving *meanings* and *relevance*.

For a cat to look at a king is for some of the king's accidental forms (his appearance) to be taken up into the nervous structure of the animal's *body* as a matter of the *relevance* of an organ, the eye, to the whole organism, the body. This I talked about earlier. Now I am going to suggest that for a human animal to have a form as understood, as a *thought*, is (roughly speaking) for this form to be taken up into the structure of *language*, as a matter of the relevance of a symbol to the whole language, the whole structure of communication that is unique to the human animal. The meaning of any word is the part it plays in, its relevance to, the whole language, as a sensation is the relevance of what goes on in a sense organ to the whole nervous system; to be able to use a word is to have a form in mind, to be able to have a thought. To have a mind is to be able to use such symbols.

That we use symbols is quite simply a fact about human animals and it seems to me the fundamental fact about them; it does not just make them into a different species of animal, as a giraffe is of a different species from a rabbit; it makes them into *animals in a new sense*—just as having sensations marks off giraffes from buttercups not just in the way that roses are different from buttercups but because giraffes (having structures of sensation) are organisms in a different sense from buttercups or roses. (Of course, I know the exact lines are hard to draw between plants and animals, but that does not seem relevant at the moment.)

Human animals are animals in a new sense for this reason. Other animals are organic bodily structures and moreover they belong organically to the greater structure which is the species; but the structures in question here are *given*. For any animal to be, to be alive, *is* for it to be structured in these particular ways. Within these structures the animal operates in terms of meanings—for meaning just is the relationship of *part* to *whole* in a *structure*. Now the human animal not only shares in much of this but it operates in structures that are *of its own making*. It is the special characteristic of the human animal that it operates in terms of structures, and thus of meanings, which are its own spontaneous creation. We are not born with language; we create it. We are born with (genetically given) a capacity for language (the right kind of body, a complex nervous system, etc.). And we learn it. Other animals are simply born with a repertoire of *signals*. We too have some 'natural gestures' but not many.

I should like at this point, if I can, to scotch a red herring. I most certainly do not want to say that human animals are like other animals in all other respects but that unlike the others they also have this special game of playing with symbols or words. I am *not* saying that lots of animals can hunt and swim and make love but the human ones can talk *as well*. Quite the contrary: I am saying that pretty well all the behaviour of human animals is significantly different from that of other animals, and if you analyse this difference you find it has to do with the human's ability to deploy symbols. I am not saying that the characteristic human thing *is* the deployment of symbols. Human animals exhibit not just what St Thomas calls theoretical intelligence in talking but also practical intelligence in behaviour. Human animals can hunt intelligently or stupidly (and this is not the same as hunting well or badly). If you try to explain what you meant by saying that someone hunted intelligently you have to say something like: it was *as though* she were saying to herself, 'If I do so and so, then ...' You are emphatically not saying that as a matter of psychological fact she *did* say these things to herself; as though acting intelligently were *both* acting *and* carrying on an internal monologue.

Now what sort of thing do you mean by saying she acted *as though* she were saying, 'If I do so and so, then . . .'? An account of what she in fact *did* might not differ much from the account of a leopard cunningly hunting, just as the account of what the leopard *did* might not differ much from what a computerized machine might seem to do. What makes the difference between her and the leopard is that you describe her actions against a background of endless other possibilities that might have been. OK, she acted just like a leopard would have done; but the leopard *had* to act like that; a leopard that did not act like that would necessarily have been a sick or defective leopard. She might have acted differently without being sick or incompetent; she might have had very good reasons; she might have *wanted* to hunt badly—she might have been bribed to do so, or she might be doing it to take the mickey out of a lot of solemn people, or any one of an indefinite number of reasons.

Now to say that she *has* reasons for acting is to say that it was *as though* she were saying certain things to herself. Of course there is a reason why the leopard hunts—he is a healthy leopard and he or his cubs are hungry; he acts for a reason. But the leopard does not *have* this reason. It is not one he proposes to himself. He just has *significant* experience in virtue of his bodily structure. But to *propose* a reason to yourself you have to do something analogous to talking. We call it thinking.

It is because the leopard cannot analyse its action in words (not just *does* not, but *cannot*) that, while it can act willingly or unwillingly, it cannot act intentionally, with an intention. The dog tearing away across the garden after the neighbour's cat is visibly acting voluntarily or willingly; you can see it and hear it barking with exuberance and joy. It is acting in accordance with its sensual structures of meaning. If you call it back and it is a well-trained dog, it will come back but again it will be equally *visibly* reluctant and unwilling. What is special about human animals is that we not only, like the dog, have things we naturally like to do, things we naturally are reluctant not to do, we can also formulate aims and intentions for ourselves. This formulation or setting of aims for ourselves can only be expressed by saying, 'We did what amounted to saying to ourselves: this is what I am trying to achieve and this is how I will achieve it.' This is different from simply *having* an aim, in that you might *not* have formulated it or set it for yourself. It is just this 'is-but-might-not-have-been' that language exists to express. Whenever I act intentionally it is always possible for you to ask me, 'What did you do that for?', 'What was the meaning of your action?', 'What was it that your act was an act of?', 'What story is it a part of?' And whatever answer I give will be informative precisely because there might have been other answers. This is the story and it might have continued differently. In the case of a dog's action, the question 'What did it do that for?' is answered by an accurate account of what it did in the context of the kind of beast that it is and the circumstances. If you get this answer right there are no other possibilities. Other answers only remain possible in the sense that you might find out more about, say, the circumstances; whatever answer you *finally* come to renders all the others not only false but impossible. This is not so with human action.

So for an adequate account of human activities it is necessary to refer to the intentions with which actions are done. As we shall be seeing later, this means asking what story the action belongs to. To have an intention is to be able to answer the question: 'Why did you do that?' It is not necessary actually to ask and answer that question either with material words or by imagining the use of material words; but it is to be *prepared to, able to,* answer the question. Of course there are a lot of things I do for which I cannot answer such a question. I may scratch my chin and I may not only be unable to say why I did it, I might not even have noticed that I did it. Again I have a whole series of operations like breathing and digesting food of which it would be senseless to ask *why* I did them. Still there are also a lot of activities, and these are the ones we think of as characteristically, uniquely human, of which we can sensibly ask: 'Why did you do that?' or 'What was that for?' or, for that matter, 'Why did you do nothing?' And this is to ask: 'Supposing you *had* actually said to yourself, "I am going to do A and this is the way I will do it", what would A have been?'— supposing, that is, that I were not only to *live* but to *narrate* my life story. This means that questions about intentions only make sense in the case of animals to whom questions can be addressed.

You can certainly speak of the reason why the dog chased the cat, but asking the dog about it does not enter into the matter. This is not just because the dog happens to be dumb but because being non-linguistic it cannot have its *own* reasons; it cannot have intentions. An intention, then, seems to be a reason for action that is my *own* reason, something I propose to myself.

That is why intentional action is the most thorough kind of self-moving or, if you like, the highest kind of vitality, of life, for any material thing. The life or soul of the linguistic animal, the one that can have intentions, is the most lively kind of life, the highest kind of soul (well, anyway, the highest we have looked at so far).

I should say, by the way, that when I say that I can have my own reasons in a way that a dog cannot have its own reasons I am not claiming that my own intentions are in some way especially clear to me. I just mean that I can try to answer your question 'Why did you do that?' whereas a dog cannot even try. I may very well fail; it may very well happen that other people know more about my intentions than I do; it is quite common for me to conceal my true intentions from myself. I may very well tell myself loudly and clearly that I am acting from the highest possible principles and a cool sense of justice, when everybody else knows perfectly well that I am acting out of resentment and wounded vanity. I am by no means the best authority on my intentions but still I can *have* intentions to be wrong about or deceive myself about; and dogs cannot.

Thoughts (meaning in a language system) are very different from sensations (meaning in the nervous system). Non-linguistic animals, and for a lot of the time linguistic animals, cannot help having the sensations they have. In a way, the world imposes sensations on the animal. This is because the meaning of the world exists in the non-linguistic animal as a conformation of its nervous system including, of course, its brain. Just as the 'meaning' of, say, the wolf (its being dangerous) exists in the wolf as a set of facts about its teeth and claws and what not, so this meaning exists in the sheep as a set of related facts about its nerves and brain, and about the relations between them. Given ordinary circumstances and ordinary healthy wolves and sheep there is no way that the dangerousness that exists in the wolf physically will not exist as sensuous meaning in the nervous system of the sheep looking at it.

Now there is a dramatic difference when we come to consider how I might come to *talk* to myself or to others about the wolf. As it happens I have never met a wolf socially, but when I do I expect to feel at least as uneasy as a sheep does. But besides accommodating the dangerousness of the wolf in the structure of my nervous system I can also accommodate it in a different way in the structure of my language. Dangerousness exists in one way in the wolf itself; in another way in my sensual experience; in yet another way in my mind as the meaning of the word 'dangerous'. The wolf is a material thing that *has* dangerousness; I have a material organic structure by which I *experience* dangerousness; the words of the English language are material things that *signify* dangerousness. Now a vital difference between the experience and the signifying is that experience is what happens to me because of the material apparatus of my nervous system, but significance is the way I *use* the material things which are words or other

49

symbols. Significance is in my use of the symbols; it is a matter of my creative activity; experience, by comparison, is passive.

We have the *sensations* we have, broadly speaking, because of the conformations in the structure of our nervous systems. We conceive the *meanings* we have not because of the physical structure of our words or of our enunciation or imagining of words, but because of the use we make of these signs in the human business of communication with each other, which lies at the heart of the human kind of society.

It seems to me quite plain that a human society is a structure in which the bits are related to the whole in ways quite unlike the ways the bits of a typewriter are related to the machine, or the ways the organs of a body are related to the whole animal, or the ways that individual animals are related to the whole species. It seems to me plain that we historically create the ways in which we relate to each other. When I say it is quite plain I mean that it does not seem to me that this is a *theory* any more than the view that daffodils die or tigers become enraged is a theory. I mean it is the kind of view that you would need a theory in order to deny. When I say the use of language is creative I am not talking just about creating new words: the use of *any* word, new or old, is creative in the sense that, say, having a fairly simple sensation is not creative. What you *see* is more or less determined by how the world is around you; what you *say* is not so determined. You may come to speak of your world in an indefinite number of ways, only contingently limited by the vocabulary available to you. It is this capacity to conceptualize the world in an indefinite number of ways and to construct an indefinite number of sentences that lies at the root of human freedom. It is because, and to the extent that, we act not simply in terms of how we have to sensually *experience* the world, but of how we *symbolize* it, that our activity is free.

Chapter 6

Narratives and Living Together

What is the special and characteristic mark of human society? The fact that human communication involves the free and creative use of symbols and the fact that human beings live together in political society are two sides of the same truth. It is because of this that a whole range of words such as 'crime', 'commitment', 'conversation', 'exploitation', 'liberation', 'loyalty', 'tradition', 'drama', and 'revolution' are used literally in accounts of this human society, though we sometimes extend them metaphorically to other animal groupings or even more remote areas. I want to concentrate on one of these concepts—the notion of story or narrative. Human beings live and live together in such a way that their lives are stories. This, I think, is not true of the existence of other animals, and it is certainly not true of machines.

I want to argue that we should think of the self in the narrative mode and recognize that narrative history of a certain kind turns out to be the basic and essential genre for the characterization of human action.[1] I shall suggest that living a *human* life, having a *human* soul, is being a character in a story, or rather in many stories, and that this belongs to being in a history or rather in many histories. I shall be

---

[1] Cf. Alasdair MacIntyre, *After Virtue* (London: Duckworth, 1981).

suggesting that life stories are not just made of words but are, so to speak, lived before they are told. In other words it is not just that we happen to be able to play the game of language, using certain material things as symbols, but our whole bodily life has a symbolic character in the sense that it is a meaningful part of a story. We live this story and sometimes we tell it to others or to ourselves—and this is called speaking and thinking.

We are not just human *beings* but human *becomings*. Like all other animals and unlike rock crystals, for us, to be is to have a lifetime, a development; but for us, and unlike for other animals, our lifetime is a life *story*. The difference is that the characters in a life story in part make their own development; they make decisions, sometimes crucial decisions, which determine how the story will go on. Human animals are to this extent *in charge* of their lifetimes, their life stories. That is why the study of human behaviour is ethics, while the study of other animal behaviour is only ethology. When *Watership Down* came out it was reviewed in the *New York Review of Books* and the writer described it as a charming tale about some middle-class English children disguised as rabbits. And so they were. You could not have a *story* about actual rabbits. Because they do not control their own stories by decisions of the human kind there could be no drama, no comedy, no tragedy, no history. Ethics, then, is just the study of human lives considered precisely as life stories. And what it is concretely to be a human being is to be a character in a life story—this is what is known as your 'self'. (This usage is not due to Aquinas.)

Whatever extra padding goes into it, the report of a football match is essentially a report on an ordered series of solutions to practical problems, problems that are being solved (or not solved) by the players on the field—not solved by talking about them to others or to themselves in their heads, but in their intelligent activity. Intelligent activity, whether in the limited and abstract area of playing football or in the complete concrete area of a human life, is not a matter, or does not have to be a matter, of first thinking something out in words (with your theoretical intelligence) and then acting on the conclusion to which you have come. Aristotle and St Thomas compare intelligent activity to a kind of reasoning in which the conclusion you come to is not a proposition in words but an action.

Of course one big difference between the game of football and the game of life is connected with the abstractness and simplicity of football. In football it is relatively simple to say what counts as successful activity, well-performed activity, because the aims and purposes of the players, as players, are easy to understand. They are easy to understand because we invented them. What counts as winning or losing, what counts as good or bad play, and also what counts as inadmissible play, has been decided (by the Football Association, let us suppose).

This does *not* seem to be the case with the game of life; nor could it be.

It is quite easy for us to understand that the point and purpose of the game of football is a matter of a decision the Football Association makes within the game of living; it is not so clear how we come by an idea of the point and purpose of the game of living itself.

To cut a long story short, because I haven't time to argue everything: Aquinas thought that the point of human living cannot lie outside human living. I mean it cannot lie outside in the way that the point of being a machine lies outside itself. Machines exist to amuse and/or be useful to human animals. The point of human living cannot be either to amuse or be useful to other animals. I think it is true and very, very importantly true that the point of human living lies *beyond* itself, but not *outside* itself. This is because I think that in the end the point of human living lies in God, who is beyond us but not outside us. God, unlike the birds or any other creatures, cannot lie outside us because he creates us and sustains us all the time, making us to be and keeping us as ourselves. So to say that the point of our lives is in God is not

53

to point to something outside us but to a greater depth within us.

However, before we come to God I would like to suggest that with human animals as with all other animals *the purpose of life is living with each other*. This means that a good and well-functioning animal, a healthy animal, is one that lives well with the rest of its species. Living well with them involves, for example, mating with them but also competing for mates and, in the case of at least one species, eating your mate after intercourse. Zoologists often remark on how extraordinarily diverse and peculiar are the various solutions that different species have evolved to the problem of surviving, but, whatever the oddity of the set-up, a healthy well-functioning shark or praying mantis is one that fits into the requirements of the species, one that lives well with its kin, according to its kind.

What distinguishes the human animal is the unique way it has found of living together. What binds the human species together, and what is thus necessary for its flourishing is not just kinship, genes, blood relationship, but culture—that whole area that arises from our capacity to create symbols, centrally of course, to use language, but we have to include music, painting, the building of cities, the development of communications of all kinds, all the technologies, arts, and sciences. It is because of all this that our lifetimes are life stories, that our lives are in our own hands.

We have, then, a special name for *human* living with each other: we call it friendship. Friendship is more than love. Friendship is more than people wishing well to other people. It involves what Aquinas calls *communicatio*, sharing, and the New Testament calls *koinonia*, sharing a common life. Friendship is a matter of being *with* others.

Now if the purpose of human living is to live with each other, and if this involves living in friendship, so that the good life for human animals is one in which friendship is fostered and preserved, this is *not* something that we have resolved upon, not a decision or option we have come to, not even a fundamental option. It is something that belongs to us because of the kind of animal we are, the linguistic or rational or symbol-making animal. We are born as players of this game; we do not *decide* what shall be its aim and purpose. We *discover* these things.

Of course discovering what kind of animals we are and what this implies takes a very long time and centuries of poetry and drama and critical philosophical thinking, and even then we are likely to make a lot of mistakes. That is why Aquinas thought it was very decent of God to help us out by giving us an outline of what it is to live in friendship: this is the Ten Commandments. God thought that we *might*, after some thought, come to the conclusion that friends would not kill each other or seduce each other's husbands or wives or get them falsely convicted of crimes or kidnap and enslave them or seek to defraud them of their possessions; yes, we might come to work that out, but all the same it would be a good idea to get all this down in black and white, or better still, on tablets of stone. Well, it wasn't quite like that: but the Decalogue *is* part of God's summons to Israel to be *his* people, to share in his life and his righteousness. God is telling them that the first step to being God's people is to be human people, and that means living in friendship. This use of human means is a minimal requirement for living beyond our means, living in the divine friendship which is God.

It is, however, important to see that what is provided by such a document as the Decalogue is precisely an *outline* of friendship. That is to say, it draws a boundary around friendship to show where it stops: beyond these limits friendship does not exist. This is the characteristic function of *law*. When I was talking about football and saying that it is our invention and that its aims and purposes are decided by the Football Association, I said that their decision in the end determined what counts as *good* or *bad play*, and also what counts as *inadmissible play*; these are two different kinds of stipulation. It is the difference between not playing football well, and not playing it at all, but perhaps pretending to. Someone who commits a foul is seeking to obtain a result which looks like winning a football match but without playing football. It is with such matters that criminal laws are characteristically concerned and they are very important, but you cannot learn how to play football well simply by knowing what such laws are, what kind of moves are inadmissible. Learning to play football well is a matter of acquiring skill by practice. For this you need the guidance of a teacher who already knows how to play well, though it may also be useful to read a book written by such a teacher. In either case you do not learn by listening to what the teacher says or by reading what he says; you learn by *practising* in accordance with what he says. If it is a matter of some complicated athletic feat or manoeuvre, you will begin by laboriously following the dotted lines in the diagram and going through the process many times, telling yourself what the next bit is. During the early stages of learning you will be listening to yourself or listening to your teacher and following the instructions. As you carry on you will gradually develop a skill; the thing will become, as they say, 'second nature' to you. This is what Aquinas calls a *habitus*—a disposition. *Habitus* does not mean habit. To be able to drive a car is a *habitus* or disposition. It means you can drive without an instructor, without constantly referring to a manual, without having to tell yourself when it is safe to overtake or when you should use your indicator. You just do these things intelligently and effortlessly. To drive skilfully in this way is not to drive out of habit in the sense that you may have a drink habit or a habit of smoking. As Anthony Kenny has put it neatly: a disposition or skill or *habitus* makes it easier for you to do what you want to do; a habit makes it harder for you not to do what you do not want to do.[2]

---

[2] Anthony Kenny, *The Metaphysics of Mind* (Oxford: Clarendon Press, 1989), p. 85.

The dispositions you need to acquire in order to play football well are skills, dispositions towards producing a good *result*, a good solution to a particular footballing problem, for example. The dispositions you need to acquire in order to play the game of life well are called virtues. It is because we are not just human beings but human becomings that we need virtues. We need dispositions that will make it easy for us to make good practical decisions in carrying on our life story. So while a skill or a technique is directed to the excellence of the thing produced, a virtue is directed to the excellence of the producer (the development of good or bad dispositions of this kind, virtues or vices, is the development of a *self*). The excellence we are concerned with when we look at human behaviour in the totally practical, totally non-abstract way that we adopt in moral judgement is not the excellence of something that *results* from a human action but the very human action *itself*. This is going to mean: is it directed towards or against the being human (or becoming human) of this human actor?; and this is going to mean in the end: is it or is it not a preservation and fostering of friendship?—that kind of friendship upon which human community and thus human existence depends. I say this is what it means in the *end*, because this is what the good life is for a human animal, but this is not what our immediate moral judgements are about. You do not criticize a move by a footballer simply by saying it is bad football, you say in what particular way his actions have failed in skill, and the skills involved in football are many and various, but nothing like as many and various as the virtues required for the good human life.

Chapter 7

Meaning, Understanding, and Making Decisions

Virtues are dispositions that have to do with our practical behaviour and so they belong to our living, which involves a complex interweaving of knowledge and desire. All desire is simply being attracted or repelled because of an *interpretation* of the world. We share with the other animals desires which arise from a sense-interpretation of the world: things are attractive or repulsive to us because of how they feel to us. But being linguistic animals we also interpret our world in terms of what can be *said* of it. To *speak* of the world is not merely to express how it makes us *feel* but how it *is* and *is not*. It is our linguistic capacity that makes us able to ask and answer *questions* and thus (with luck) to grasp *truth*, to escape from the subjectivity and privacy of feeling into objectivity. And this is because linguistic meanings do not *belong* to anyone in the way that feelings do; meanings are in the language, which is of its nature public and common. So while nobody could have my sensations, only more or less similar ones, everyone must be able to have my thoughts. It is most unlikely that you have exactly the same sensations and emotions as I have in drinking a pint of Guinness, but we all mean exactly the same by the linguistic expression 'drinking a pint of Guinness' because this meaning is not in any one of us but in the English language. As Aquinas sees it, understanding a meaning is transcending our privacy, our subjectivity, our individuality, our materiality. We share with each other, communicate with each other in terms of truth, in ways which are not simply individual and bodily, by the use of signs and symbols to express meanings.

It seems to me that if we take seriously Wittgenstein's argument that there can be no such thing as a private language a conclusion follows from this which Wittgenstein himself, so far as I know, never drew. Aquinas, however, starting from a rather similar premiss, the clear distinction between individual, material, bodily sensation and non-individual understanding, does draw it. Wittgenstein's position is not to be confused with, say, behaviourism. Behaviourists deny that we can meaningfully talk of private occurrences in my mind or 'inside my head'. Behaviourists think that all that we can scientifically know about people is their external behaviour. Now Wittgenstein does not deny that I may have, for example, mental images or for that matter concepts. What he is asserting is that such inner events are not what gives meaning to my words. He would be perfectly happy to say that the individual Fred has a concept of what a horse is, but he would, I think, say (and I would certainly say) that to have such a concept is to have a skill, a *habitus*, a skill, though not a bodily skill, in using this word 'horse'; but the meaning of the word is not its relation to my concept but its place in the structure of a language. Of course the *use* of a word involves bodily skills in speaking or writing; but these are not the skills of the concept. The *meaning* of a word is not *mine* in the sense that *my having* this skill, this concept, *is* mine and not yours: the mind which is my capacity for this skill is part of the vitality of this body, not that one; the meaning, though, belongs not to me but to the English language. The meaning of a word, although I may have it in mind, is not mine in the sense that my walking is mine. Nobody can have my walking, but anybody and everybody can have my thought, because it is not private to me.

What Aquinas and Wittgenstein have in common in this

matter is that both are concerned to criticize a doctrine which assimilates meanings or concepts to sensations. Aquinas thought that one of Aristotle's greatest achievements was to make a clear division between the two and to conclude that understanding a meaning could not be a bodily operation—however much it needs the concurrence of bodily events (*phantasmata*), as is shown by the fact that linguistic intellectual life is impeded by some bodily conditions such as being drunk.

Wittgenstein's target is the empiricist tradition most clearly set forth by David Hume (we have seen some of what follows before):

All the perceptions of the human mind resolve themselves into two distinct kinds, which I shall call IMPRESSIONS and IDEAS. The difference betwixt these consists in the degrees of force and liveliness, with which they strike upon the mind, and make their way into our thought or consciousness. Those perceptions, which enter with most force and violence, we may name *impressions*; and under this name I comprehend all our sensations, passions and emotions, as they make their first appearance in the soul. By *ideas* I mean the faint images of these in thinking and reasoning; such as, for instance, are all the perceptions excited by the present discourse, excepting only, those which arise from the sight and touch, and excepting the immediate pleasure or uneasiness it may occasion. I believe it will not be very necessary to employ many words in explaining this distinction. Every one of himself will readily perceive the difference betwixt feeling and thinking. The common degrees of these are easily distinguished; tho' it is not impossible but in particular instances they may very nearly approach to each other. Thus in sleep, in a fever, in madness, or in any very violent emotions of soul, our ideas may approach to our impressions: As on the other hand it sometimes happens, that our impressions are so faint and low, that we cannot distinguish them from our ideas. But notwithstanding this near resemblance in a few instances, they are in general so very different, that no-one can make a scruple to rank them under distinct heads, and assign to each a peculiar name to mark the difference.[1]

The difference Hume is referring to is a difference between the force and liveliness of sensation and the faintness of their images which are 'ideas', and this Wittgenstein thinks just won't do.

The notion that we explain the meaning of a word by referring to an idea in my head (and one that I hope but cannot establish is in your head) really assimilates concepts to sensations, which do exist in my nervous system as a complex structure of relationships between various organs of the body. Wittgenstein detaches meaning from the hidden interior workings of my psychology and places it in the public sphere of language. This removal of meanings from the field of operations by individual, materially distinct animals, is, in Aquinas's way of speaking, to remove it from materiality, for *materia* is the principle of individuality.

To put it summarily, both Wittgenstein and Aquinas would agree that I can say, 'This is what it *feels like for me*'; and both would agree that you cannot say, 'This is what the word "hallucinatory" *means for me*.' A word has its meaning not in any material individual but in the language, which transcends individuality and thus transcends matter. Of course a language is itself a material thing made of sounds or visual patterns, but it is with the meanings of these material symbols that we are concerned.

Aquinas's argument is different from Wittgenstein's, but the point is that they both come to the same conclusion: that you misread linguistic life if you assimilate it to sensations or to

[1] David Hume, *A Treatise of Human Nature*, ed. L. A. Selby-Bigge, 2nd edn (Oxford: Clarendon Press, 1978), pp. 1–2.

whatever exists in the nervous system (events in the brain, for example).

Averroës (ibn-Rushd) was a somewhat neo-Platonist Aristotelian so impressed by the non-privacy of meanings he thought they existed not in the language but in a single separate mind. For their own reasons Aristotle and Aquinas said that understanding has no corporeal organ, in the way that seeing requires a change in the eye, or hearing a change in the ear, etc.[2] Of course to *acquire* my concepts I have to be sensually engaged with the world. Interpreting the world linguistically, involving it in language, depends on first interpreting it sensually, involving it in the nervous system. Moreover Aquinas is explicit that when I use a word or make use in any way of my understanding I need in some way to return to the interior sense he calls *imaginatio*: the interior bodily sense of what it is like to be sensually aware of the world. There has to be a 'return', as he would say, 'to the *phantasmata*'. Nevertheless, to *have* a concept in the under-standing (to have learnt and not forgotten what, say, 'hallucinatory' or 'custard' means) is not to undergo some modification of your nervous system or any part of your body. It is true that if you have forgotten, this may be due to some malfunctioning of the interior senses which would ordinarily accompany recall, but understanding the concept is not *itself* an affair of the interior senses but of the mind, the capacity for linguistic meaning. Now from the fact that understanding is not a physical act of this or any other individual material body—the fact that in understanding, in our use of language, we can transcend our material individuality—Aquinas argues that our life is not exhausted by our bodily life. There is more to my life than what goes on in my body.

The grin of a Cheshire cat is an accidental *form* of the cat, and it would be nonsense to speak of the grin remaining when

---

[2] Aristotle, *De Anima*, 3, 4; Aquinas, *Commentary on De Anima*, 3, 7; *Summa Theologiae*, 1a, 75.

the cat has faded away. Similarly the life of the Cheshire cat is also a form, the substantial form, of the cat—what it takes for the cat to be in the first place. And again it would be nonsense to speak of the substantial form of the cat remaining after the cat has gone. What *subsists*, Aquinas says, is the *cat*, which is some matter informed by a particular kind of life. Neither the matter nor the form can subsist separately. So all the vital operations of the cat are vital operations of this material cat's body. The whole cat *contains*, you might say, its matter and its form. The form is contained in the whole cat and if there is no cat there, the form is not there. There is, however, a difference, argues Thomas, between the non-linguistic and the linguistic animal, between brute beasts and rational animals, because linguistic animals have an operation which is not a corporeal one. Its vital operations include *thought*, which cannot be bodily. So here what subsists is the life itself. For the life or soul of the linguistic animal, so to say, extends beyond its bodily capacities. In this, the human, case we should speak of the life or soul containing the body as just *one* range of its operations. The human soul is rather containing than contained in the whole person.

I think it is important to recognize that Aquinas's argument has merely shown that there is not the same kind of nonsense in saying that a human life is not limited to its corporeal activity as there would be in saying the same of the life of a cat. He has not argued that we can have any *concept* of a human life which is not bodily engaged. And this is entirely consistent with his view that human understanding, which has as its material, so to say, our sensual interpretation of the world, can only receive the forms of material sensible things. We cannot, for Aquinas, understand what an angel is, because it is immaterial; still less, of course, can we understand what God is—until we are taken up into his own self-understanding in heaven, when we shall know him not by any human concept but as he knows himself in his Word.

It is all a lot easier, at least at first sight, for non-Aristotelian dualists who think that in human animals there are two linked substances, a body and a soul, such that when the body dies the soul detaches itself from bodily limitations and expresses itself more fully and happily in heaven. You can see how this kind of Platonism has had an immediate appeal to Christians and why a thoroughgoing Aristotelian like Aquinas should have been held in such suspicion by respectable clerics. At the funeral of the great Christian Socialist mayor of Oxford, Olive Gibbs, I heard the clergyman say that we were only burying the remains of her body but her 'real self' was elsewhere. Aquinas thought otherwise: *Anima mea non est ego*, he said (My soul is not me, not my self). But then, of course, he believed in the resurrection of the body.

That we have no concept of what Aquinas calls the 'separated soul' does not prevent us (or him) from talking about it, just as the fact that we do not know what God is does not prevent us from talking about him. In fact Aquinas says quite a lot about the knowledge that such a soul could have even though there is no body to supply the *phantasmata* which he thinks of as necessary for (though not part of) human understanding. For myself, I believe, as a matter of Catholic faith, that we can ask the saints to pray for us, so their separated souls (which is all there is of them in heaven) must know about our prayers to them. But for me this is a mystery I do not expect to or even try to explain. The problem, of course, does not arise either with the risen Christ himself or with Mary assumed into heaven, both of whom are proper bodily animals (however 'glorified').

But back to this life. To have language is to be able to know the truth about the world, and, of course, by the same token, to make mistakes about it. What we feel is just what we feel, and there is no way of 'correcting' it except medically; but what we *say* of the world is open to discussion with others and within ourselves. Using our intelligence, talking about the world (unlike seeing the world), is a *task*, a work of investigation, something we have to *do*.

And we may or may not want to do it. For just as our sense-knowledge gives rise to desires (we are attracted or not by what we sense), so does our rational knowledge, our linguistic way of interpreting the world. And the thing about this linguistic interpretation is that it isn't simply *there* like a sensation.

A hungry dog seeing a juicy steak, unless it is sick, cannot but desire it, and cannot but try to act on this desire—unless specially trained, in which case it cannot but *not* try to act. It can only be aware of the steak under the aspect of its delightful smell and pleasant appearance. But we are aware of things not just in terms of their sensible appearance but also *under a description*, in fact under an indefinite number of descriptions. We are not only attracted by the smell etc.; we also recognize the steak as, for example, belonging to somebody else, being produced by the slaughter of harmless beasts, high in cholesterol, extremely expensive, ... and so on. All these are thoughts or considerations about the steak, and plainly they could go on indefinitely.

How much we will think about the matter is (in part) a matter of how much we want to. For considering something is a human activity and any human activity, including thinking, is done because we want to do it, because we find it attractive, or at least not repulsive, to do it.

Suppose that my neighbour's wife and I are passionately attracted to each other and wish to go to bed together. Of course I know quite well at one level that she is my neighbour's wife but there is a difference between *knowing* something and *considering* it, bringing it before my mind—just as you knew five minutes ago how to spell your name, that Liverpool is north of London, that the Lord's Prayer is also called the Our Father, that $17 + 5 = 22$, but, I like to think, you had something else in mind and were not paying any especial attention to these pieces of knowledge at the time. Now it is quite possible for me to find the thought of my neighbour's wife as my beloved an unpleasant one to contemplate, and so I can push it to the back of my mind where it does not provide a motive for action (or inaction). In this way I can be motivated to do what in one sense I know quite well to be irrational and wrong, and which, on later consideration, I will acknowledge to be such. It is, as I have said, our linguistic capacity to understand things and situations under an indefinite number of descriptions that in St Thomas's view is the root of human freedom, the root of our capacity to make actions really our own, flowing from our own decision, and also of course the root of our capacity to deceive ourselves and behave irrationally, and badly.

In the story I have been telling about my alleged sex life, what was missing, of course, was a good education. If I had only acquired by education certain elementary virtues, things would have happened differently. What I needed was, for example, the virtue of temperateness in my emotional life and this is not a matter of my *will*, my rational appetite, but of my physical bodily desires and emotions, so that I would not be simply overwhelmed by sexual attraction but keep it in its proper place amongst many other aspects of human living. I would also need the virtue of justice, which is a matter of my rational appetite, cool rational assessment, so that I just naturally took account of what was owing both to my beloved and to her husband; I would be reluctant to exploit her affection for me, and reluctant to deceive him and make their marital life even more difficult than most marital lives are. The result of acquiring such virtues would be that I would have had a truer view of the situation; I would be considering the important things about it and not the good, but relatively trivial good, to be attained by going to bed with her, or anyway not concentrating exclusively on this relatively trivial good.

But above and beyond such moral virtues as temperateness and justice, I would need to have acquired the virtue of good sense, or *prudentia*. This is not reckoned by St Thomas among the moral virtues because it has to do directly not with desires and emotions, but with understanding. He says it is an intellectual virtue, but since it is concerned with the practical intellect it is all tied up with the virtues that govern desires as well. And without it there can be no true moral virtues. Good sense is the virtue, or rather cluster of virtues, that makes it easy and 'second nature' to us to make good decisions. Good sense is a kind of clear-sightedness about our problems which enables us to put them in proper perspective, to see what is more important and what is less so. It also, and most importantly, involves a certain clear-sightedness about my self. And it involves not just the mind, understanding, but sensual engagement with the world, sensitivity.

Like St Augustine, St Thomas speaks of free choice, *liberum arbitrium*, and not, as later writers did, of free *will*. For them, freedom was a mysterious property of the will. I have even read people suggesting that Heisenberg's Uncertainty Principle made free will more plausible, because of the randomness and unpredictability introduced into physics. For Aquinas the will is, of course, operative in choice but the choice is free because the will is attracted by what is *understood* to be in some way or other good. So unless it be confronted by sheer goodness itself, which is God (whom in any case we cannot understand in this life), the will may have a variety of reasons for being attracted; and thus the choice or decision is free. For Aquinas we are free not because we act at random or unpredictably, but because we act for reasons, and there are many possible available reasons. Which reasons we will plump for has to do with what we have made of ourselves—our virtues or vices.

When Aristotle talks of choice, decision (*prohairesis*), he speaks of exercising an 'appetitive intelligence' or an 'intelligent appetite'. For Aquinas, in my view, this applies to every stage in human action. At no point in the exercise of practical reason are intellect and will separated. There is no act of practical intelligence which is not also one of will, and vice versa. Aquinas likes to say that the two are not like two powers side by side but are united as form and matter, though exchanging these roles continually.

To go back to what I was saying earlier, a game such as football has two quite different kinds of limitations on its players: they should play the game *well* and they should not *cheat*. They should be first concerned with dispositions (skills), second with individual acts. Learning to play well is analogous to acquiring a virtue or virtues; an act of cheating, which is attempting to win without playing the game at all, but pretending to while doing something else, is analogous to sin. A certain kind of law which absolutely prohibits certain *acts* has the function of listing various common methods of cheating.

Such laws define the boundaries of the game. From the point of view of moral philosophy the game is friendship (*philia*) in the sense in which Aristotle described it as that relationship by which people are fellow-citizens; and it is more than justice. Justice is the minimum proper relationship with foreigners, but, in addition to this, citizenship demands a concern for the flourishing of your friends, a concern, therefore, for their virtues and their concern for my virtues. Friendship is both the aim of all the virtues and also the necessary means by which virtues are cultivated, sustained, and developed. Virtues can only be taught by friends. Friendship can only be sustained by virtues. (There is a fashion at the moment among those who believe in what they call the market economy for what Aristotle would regard as treating citizens as though they were foreigners.) That's moral *philosophy*, but from the point of view of moral *theology* the *philia* which defines the game is *agape* or *caritas*, the friendship that God shares with us and enables us to share with each other. A table of prohibitions such as the Decalogue defines the *boundaries* of *caritas*: to break them is not to play the game poorly but to step outside the field of play. And to return it is not a simple matter of learning to play better. You need gratuitous forgiveness, Good News.

Of course, being thoroughly familiar with laws does not help you to play well—indeed it is quite compatible with never playing the game at all. It is an exercise of theoretical intelligence rather than practical intelligence.

To play the game well we need, not rule books, but training. We may at first make use of training manuals or teachers, but we do not acquire the skill we need by reading the books or listening to the teachers, but by practising in accordance with their teaching. Practising has a twofold effect: you acquire a sensitivity and insight into the demands of the situation you are in, and, simultaneously, become more attracted to dealing with it in the best way. As you get better at playing you become more enthusiastic about the game. This is the combined operation of practical intelligence and will.

Of course, acquiring a skill is not the same as acquiring a virtue, for two reasons. In the first place, skill is concerned with the good of what is *produced*—a good move in football, or an excellent painting, or whatever; whereas a virtue is concerned with the excellence of the *producer*. But, interlinked with this, the second difference is that skills are acquired *only* by practice (although some people may be genetically provided with a certain natural talent which makes it much easier for them to acquire the skill—think of Mozart), but virtues which enable us to live the life of *caritas*, which is the life of God, life in the Spirit, although they encourage us to more intensive practice, are rooted not in our efforts but in the initiative of God—this is what we mean by God sharing his life with us. This is what is traditionally called 'infused' as distinct from 'acquired' virtue. The divine, or so-called 'theological', virtues of faith, hope, and charity can only be infused through the grace of God, but this grace also gives a new dimension to, and indeed transforms, our acquired virtues. As Aquinas puts it, the charity we *have* becomes the *form of all our virtues*, and our whole life becomes a sharing in divinity.

Chapter 8

Emotions and Inclinations

EMOTIONS

I now turn to look at what Aquinas calls the *passiones animae*, the 'passions of the soul', which I shall call emotions (though 'reactions' might be better).

In looking at Aquinas on the emotions it is clear how different his whole outlook is from that of pretty well all European philosophers from Descartes until Wittgenstein. The difference is that he did not hold a dualist view of human nature; he did not hold, that is, that to be human is to be two distinct substances, a material body and a non-material soul.[1] The soul for him is the life of this body—what makes it a body instead of an inanimate mechanical lump of matter. When he speaks of the 'passions of the soul' and in fact argues that the *passiones* are *in* the soul, Aquinas has no notion to deny that they are bodily (as, say, a Cartesian would have done had he said this); he means that in considering them we are considering the whole person and not just an abstraction from it that we might call 'the body as such'.

Thus when he says that an emotion, such as fear, is 'in the soul' he means that we cannot treat of it as we can, say, a broken ankle or a suntan, without any necessary reference to the whole of our vital activity. So a doctor may bind up my

---

[1] *Summa Theologiae*, 1a2ae, 22, 1.

ankle or put lotion on my sunburn without any regard to my feelings or emotions. Fear is a bodily emotion in the soul, just as hearing or smelling is a bodily perception in the soul. We can study the physiology of fear (the secretion of adrenalin or whatever) just as we can study the physiology of seeing (the changes in rods and cones etc.) and it seems that we may at last have found out how we detect smells, and Aquinas would say that in doing so we are looking at what is 'material' to fear or to seeing or to smelling. But to understand what fearing or seeing is in its totality, what makes them to be fearing or seeing or smelling, we have to understand what these physiological events *count as* for the life (the *anima* or soul) of the animal, their *meaning* in the whole animal. We have first to ask a scientific question; then we have to ask a philosophical one.

If being afraid were like breaking an ankle we might investigate what brought it on. The investigation would be simply an empirical one. I mean your ankle might have been broken by a flying stone, a slip on the ice, or a passing car. You might have to go and find out what, as a matter of contingent fact, caused the break. But Aquinas, surely rightly, holds that being afraid is *not* like that. Being afraid is brought on not by a *cause* but by an *object*, by what it is that you are afraid *of*. Compare Wittgenstein: 'We should distinguish between the object of fear and the cause of fear. Thus a face which inspires fear or delight (the object of fear or delight), is not on that account its cause, but—one might say—its target.'[2]

It would be quite unsurprising if someone said she had a broken ankle but did not know what had caused it; it would be strange if she said she was afraid but had no idea what she was afraid of. Fear, as philosophers would say, is 'intentional', it goes out to an object. As Aquinas would say: it is defined, its meaning is established, by its object.

Now it is *possible* for someone to say that, oddly enough, she

---

[2] Ludwig Wittgenstein, *Philosophical Investigations*, tr. G. E. M. Anscombe (Oxford: Basil Blackwell, 1968), §476.

is afraid but has no idea what she is afraid of; but what she means, I think, is that she experiences the physiological changes that normally belong to fear but they have been brought about by some other means. She means that she feels as though she were afraid. This is odd but not uncommon. A large constituent of a hangover, after all, is a sense of guilt which does not seem to be guilt for anything in particular.

Just as it would be very odd if someone claimed to be afraid but unaware of what she was afraid of, so too it would be extremely strange if she claimed to be afraid while she was laughing gaily and drinking champagne while executing a complex step dance, and even more strange to say, 'Can't you see she's afraid, she is laughing ...' etc. It could happen, of course: she might be a beautiful spy deliberately concealing her terror to deceive the Gestapo agent.

Fear does not *consist* of its bodily manifestations in sweating and trembling (as behaviourists used to think); but neither does it consist in some cool intellectual assessment of the situation, its 'object', as dangerous, or simply some unwillingness to have something happen to you. It is, in Aquinas's language, a bodily response of the soul (a response to what is perceived as impending bodily harm that is going to be difficult to avoid).

The passions, or emotions, then, are the bodily excitements associated with our sensual appetites. (Aquinas does recognize a delight and a love associated with the rational appetite, the will—the purely intellectual joy, for example, in suddenly seeing the point of an argument or the solution to a crossword clue; but he does not see this as constituted by a bodily excitation and so he does not reckon it an emotion.)

INCLINATIONS

Following Aristotle, Aquinas makes a broad distinction in the world of our sensual experience: there is the world as *affecting* us (the world as 'undemanding') and there is the world as needing to be *dealt with* (the world as demanding, *ardus*). This latter experience arises, he says, from the vulnerability of living things.

We read, 'In natural corruptible things there has to be not only a tendency towards what is beneficial and away from what is harmful, there also has to be a resistance to contrary and destructive forces, which threaten them or stand in the way of what they need'.[3] So like Konrad Lorentz and other ethologists Aquinas sees aggression to be just as natural as desire to all higher animals. But unlike them (especially unlike people like Robert Ardrey and Desmond Morris) he does *not* see aggression as some kind of basic behaviour which will be carried on as a matter of course unless restrained. He thinks (with most scientists these days, I think) that aggression is a natural response to certain circumstances—they usually instance food shortage and overcrowding; Aquinas merely notes that what animals need to fight about is food and sex. For him an animal, including a human animal, that lacked the appropriate aggressive response to dangers and difficulties would be defective and unhealthy.

So the sensual appetites (sensuality) can be divided into those of simple desire and those of aggression. Aquinas argues that we have to make a real distinction here because these appetites sometimes conflict: the appetite to fight interferes with our sensual desire for peace and comfort, and vice versa. It is quite important to see that the broad division into appetites of desire and aggression is a matter of our inclinations as *desirers* and as *fighters*, not a matter of whether we are confronted by what is desirable or what is undesirable—what is nice and what is nasty. As *desirers*, as wanters, we respond to *both* what is nice and what is nasty—we seek the one and avoid the other. Similarly as *fighters* we react to *both* what is nice and what is nasty, we make an effort, struggle, *for* one and *against* the other—attack/defence. The division rests not on whether

---

[3] *Summa Theologiae*, 1a, 81, 2.

what we are confronted with is seen as good or bad, but on whether or not it is difficult, making demands on us. Our aggressive appetites are concerned with what does make this kind of demand on us, our desiring attitudes with what does not. For Aquinas, as for Aristotle, the living being is the living becoming, with all its tendencies.

Aquinas's own technical terminology is based on the Latin translation of Aristotle available to him. For the appetite of desire he (adjectivally) uses *concupiscibilis* (Greek *epithumetike*; modern English, 'concupiscence') and for appetite of aggression *irascibilis* (Greek *thumike*; modern English, 'irascible'). Remember that what we are classifying here under inclinations following on what is apprehended (forms present intentionally) are *appetites*, which are capacities to be moved, passive capacities which however are the roots of action. It is because something is presented to us, or we present it to ourselves, as attractive that we act to attain it.

These appetites are good, God-given, means to happiness and ultimately divine life. They are not to be suppressed (contrary to the Stoics) but integrated, kept in order, kept in suitable relation to each other and to our overall good, which is the object of the rational appetite—*voluntas*—whose object is goodness in itself. So it is that our different bodily emotions, under the guidance of their own emotional virtues and of our overall rational inclination to our happiness, do not get out of hand but remain in reasonable harmony with other aspects of our life. This is the province of the sensual virtues of *temperateness* and *courage* respectively. Without these virtues (as we have seen) our life stories will be the continuing struggle against 'weakness of will'.

Other animals do not need such virtues, or any other virtues, because they are (and have to be) genetically tuned to the kind of lives they lead—if they are not, their species quickly perishes. For them, all appetites are a bit like natural tendencies for us. It is, I suppose, because the human animal creates so much of its own environment and circumstances that, in important areas, we lack this genetic tuning. We are not born with an instinctive capacity to survive in cities or to handle rifles. *Our* passions, both of desire and aggression, are triggered in ways for which we have no instinctive genetic provision; we need to *learn* how to cope with this. That is why *we* have ethics, how to behave *in future*, and *other* animals only have ethology, how they have always behaved. The very capacity that enables us to *build up* an artificial environment, the city, the *polis* (our language and thinking), also enables us to learn how to *cope with it*—though with difficulty and with many mistakes. Because he saw human beings as fundamentally destined to divine life, Aquinas shared the Augustinian tradition which associated the fact that we do not seem to be naturally, by birth, adjusted to the world we live in with the rejection of that divine life, with absence of grace, with original sin. Our maladjustment to *each other*—the difficulty we have and the mistakes we make in coping with the human environment we have made—is rooted in a maladjustment to the *divine*. So for Aquinas (though not of course for Aristotle) we need a restoration of our divine life; we need grace, even to cope with living a human life fully, and of course this restoration of divine life which entails the theological virtues is itself purely and entirely a gift from God.

Aquinas's detailed account of emotions is both practical and subtle as well as extremely positive. He insists that the effective way of dealing with depression is not so much to avoid what is unpleasant as to seek what is pleasant. More real harm is done by not having enough delight and enjoyment in your life than by having unpleasant things happening to you. He also recommends that if you are suffering from depression you should take a hot bath, and (as they used to say at one time in every Hollywood film) 'try to get some sleep'; and his reason is that these, being conducive to relaxed sensual pleasure, restore the body to its proper vital activity.[4]

---

[4] *Summa Theologiae*, 1a2ae, 38, 5.

The treatment of the emotions associated with the aggressive appetites (the *appetitus irascibilis*) is rather more complex. First of all there is a similar division between the world as nice and the world as nasty, but the aggressive appetites are concerned with what is difficult (the *arduum*, the arduous) so these come into play when the world as nice presents itself as difficult to attain, or the world as nasty presents itself as difficult to avoid. Taking the case of the pleasant that has to be worked for or fought for, Aquinas recognizes that we could have two different kinds of emotion with respect to it. When *what immediately strikes us* about the difficult thing (say, getting to the top of a mountain) is first of all that it is *pleasant* we have a certain exhilaration in overcoming the difficulties, and this is the emotion he calls *spes*. (This word would ordinarily be translated as 'hope' and there is a certain analogy between its use for the emotion of exhilaration in overcoming difficulties and its use for the theological virtue of hope, which a theologian would see as a kind of exhilaration in journeying through the difficulties of life towards the Kingdom.) When, however, *what immediately strikes us* about the pleasant thing is how *difficult* or perhaps impossible it is going to be (e.g. to get the goodies in the shop window because we have no money), then we are overcome with the emotion of frustration, *desperatio*. Both these emotions concern pleasant things that you are seeking, that you have not yet attained. There is of course no *aggressive* emotion concerning (no wanting to fight for) a pleasant thing that has been attained. What you do then is delight in it (*gaudium*).

Let us look now at our aggressive emotions with regard to what is undesirable and unpleasant—the nasty things that are going to be hard to avoid, that will overwhelm us unless we struggle, or which already have overwhelmed us. Here we get the same distinction between those unpleasant impending situations which strike us first of all as *dreadful* (of which we are frightened: our emotion is *timor*, fear) and, on the other hand, those that strike us first as something to be *fought*. In the latter case our emotion is one of *audacia*, militancy. Just as when we are passive to the world and are confronted with the unpleasant we pass from dislike through aversion to depression, so when we are actively trying to ward off evil we pass from fear of it through militancy to it and (when we are defeated and the evil is unavoidable) anger, *ira*. All that is left to us now is the desire for revenge and this, according to Aquinas, is what anger is. For such a mild and academic man he is quite startlingly interested in anger: he sees it as a desire for the pleasure of revenge and in that sense a matter of the appetites of *desire*, but excited by failure to ward off an evil and thus a matter for the *aggressive* appetites. He follows Aristotle in seeing it as the most 'reasonable' of the emotions in that it excites us to act for a reason (*because* of the injury suffered); it is the emotion most involved with rational assessment of the world, and Aquinas also regards it as especially natural to us. His whole analysis of anger is subtle, complex, surprising, and well worth reading[5] but too long to go into.

It must be remembered that for Aquinas the emotions are good and God-given, and he certainly regards anger as in itself a good thing. He argues that it is an emotion we need if we are effectively to exercise the virtue of *fortitudo*, courage, in defence of justice.[6] In general, he thinks, human goodness *requires* an emotional commitment. So, for Aquinas, the good life is a passionate life. It is not achieved by the repression of emotion but by emotion guided by virtues. It is to these virtues that we now at last turn.

---

[5] See *Summa Theologiae*, 1a2ae, 46–8.
[6] *Summa Theologiae* 1a2ae, 46, 6.

Chapter 9

Action, Deliberation, and Decision

It has occurred to me that what I would like to say about St Thomas's account of the human dispositions we call virtues and vices would be a lot clearer if we go back and take a look at his previous account of the psychology of human action. This is to be found in questions 12–17 of the *Summa Theologiae*'s Prima Secundae, which is not the easiest bit of the *Summa* to follow—and especially not if you read it in the manner of a 'neo-Thomist' keen to emphasize how complex and subtle it is. It is indeed subtle but not excessively complicated if you sort it out carefully. The first and most important thing to say about it is that by the time Aquinas came to write this part of the *Summa* he had just written his commentary on Aristotle's *De Anima* and come to see the whole matter much more clearly than he had done when, for example, writing his early *Commentary on the Sentences*. And what he had come to see was that when we come to the field of human action there is no operation of the reason which is not also an operation of the will, and vice versa. There is an interweaving of understanding and being attracted that cannot be unravelled in practice. We think of what we are *attracted* to thinking of, and we are attracted to what we *think* of.[1]

---

[1] I do not mean we *believe* what we want to *believe*, though this is a vice we have to be careful to avoid. I mean that we *pay attention* to what we *want to attend to*. And that aspect we present to ourselves as good is what attracts us.

As Aquinas says, you can no more separate them into two things than you could separate a living animal into body and soul. Frequently he asks: is 'intending' or 'deciding' or whatever an act of intellect or will?, and he usually answers: 'Both, but one predominantly.' It is important to see here that St Thomas is not, at this point, talking about morality, about what makes acts good or bad, but simply about psychology—about how the human animal operates. So let us get to basics:

> We *aim* at some end (we find it attractive).
> We *decide* on the means to attain it (and on the particular means that we want to use).
> We *act*.

This process is a piece of practical reasoning, a bit like a syllogism in theoretical reason, but instead of concluding in a statement, its conclusion is an action.

Aiming at the end is what Aquinas calls *intentio* and this is being attracted by some good presented to us by our understanding. It is an actualization of our capacity to be attracted that is aroused by our linguistic interpretation of the world 'taking it up into the structure of language'. I say this because we can also be attracted, as can other, non-linguistic animals, by a good presented in our sensual interpretation of the world 'taking it up into the structure of the nervous system'. But that would not be what Aquinas calls an intention. Intention is specific to the linguistic animal. I use the word 'linguistic' here because if I used Aquinas's more common phrase, 'rational appetite', it might confuse us because often, for us, and indeed for Aquinas too, 'rational' is an evaluative word—'rational activity' sounds like 'reasonable' (and thus good) activity—but that is not what is meant here. Aquinas is simply talking about action done for an aim, a *reason*: intentional action.

To have an aim is to want something; it is to have an appetite tending towards something you find attractive. Let us say you want a drink. Now this may be simply a natural desire for drink because you are very dry. This is an instinctive sensual desire that we share with other animals. In such a case you do not have an intention, simply a *thirst*. But the linguistic animal can take up her thirst into a complex linguistic interpretation of her world. She can relate it to other things to be said about it like 'Here is someone else actually dying of thirst' and 'There's only one bottle left,' or 'How much money do I have?' And, of course, she may want (intend) a drink without any sensual thirst at all ... and so on and so on. After all these considerations she reckons that she still wants to have a drink—not in some abstract sense in which, after all, we all want a drink all the time, but here and now. And so she forms the intention of getting a drink. Now this intention is, Aquinas argues, in itself an act of the will, it is a being *attracted*—and the will is nothing but our capacity to be attracted by what we think about.

The very fact that it is an act of will means that the understanding is involved, indeed presupposed. The intention of having a drink depends on an *apprehensio*, an interpretation, an account of the world rationally or linguistically. Otherwise it is a mere sensual thirst. But we must not think of two instants, one the operation of the intellect presenting some-thing attractive and the next an operation of the will being attracted. It is a single complex operation involving both will and intellect, for of course you will not actively attend to some aspect of having a drink if you don't *want* to; so the understanding bit presupposes the will as well. Think of the business of having an intention not as a kind of dry mechanical clicking back and forth between will and intellect but rather something as fluid as the drink you are going to have, something electronic but more so.

Aquinas asks whether intention is an *actus* of the will but we ought to be careful about this. An *actus* is, for him, simply the actualizing of a potentiality, so that something that *could* be, actually *is*. Now this need not be what in English we call an act: a kick or a shout or hiccup (since drink has been our topic); an *actus* can be a movement of some power or capacity to an actual *state* that was previously only *possible*. And in the case of intention, I think this is always the way it is. You are not performing an *action* of wanting a drink; you come to be in a *state* of wanting a drink, which you were not in before (perhaps you were asleep or distracted or something).

There is not an action or event of intending which is then followed by something else; there is an entering into a *state* of intending which *sets the stage* for something else.

This seems to me a very interesting way of putting it. I do not remember any text of St Thomas in which he says precisely so, but I think it is entirely in accordance with his thinking to compare having an *intention* in the field of human *action* with understanding *what something is* in the field of *theoretical* reason. He says frequently that some sort of understanding, however vague or fragmentary, of what something is, its essence—some kind of attempt to make a statement about it in the category of *substance*, saying what it is—is a necessary preliminary to knowing anything else about it. The reason for this is that unless you know, however vaguely, what sort of thing it is you are talking about, you will not know what sentences concerning it make sense and what are nonsense. If two people are wholly at cross purposes about their topic of discussion (if, being slightly deaf, I think you are talking about hamsters when in fact you are talking about amateurs), then there is no way in which we can even disagree, never mind agree. So settling what it is we are talking about—knowing, however roughly, its essence, or providing some sort of definition, however inadequate—*sets the stage* for talking (and maybe disagreeing) about the facts. We get nowhere in scientific theoretical understanding without such a preliminary setting of the stage: this is the context within which we are talking. And, as it has now suddenly occurred to me, Aquinas is saying that within the field of practical reasoning we get nowhere without formulating an intention, which sets the stage for deliberation. On this stage there may be enacted an immediate decision about what is to be done, but very often there is a preliminary deliberation: what are the best available ways to achieve this end? But in any case without articulating an intention, something we are aiming at, setting the stage, none of this can get off the ground.

'Decision' is, I think, the best English word for what Aristotle called *prohairesis* and Aquinas called *electio*. And this is the culmination of practical rationality. For Aquinas, as for Aristotle, human action is, above all, rational action. Please notice, again, that this does not mean 'reasonable' (i.e. good) action but simply the characteristic action of a linguistic animal, an animal with reason or understanding. Human animals characteristically do things for reasons that they have. Other animals do things for a reason but do not have this reason themselves as the motive of their action. The reasons available to them are genetically provided in their DNA. So if you decide to murder your aunt in order to inherit her wealth, that is, in the present relevant sense, a rational action (but not, surely, a reasonable one). Whereas the hawk who drops from the sky because he has seen a rabbit below does not do this because he reckons that this is a good reason for diving but because he is programmed so to act in those circumstances. But human actions are all of them rational though some, like murdering your aunt, are only what Aquinas would call reasonable *secundum quid*, in a certain respect—given that you have an aim of inheriting your aunt's wealth (which, for you, overrides any other consideration). We come to the *morality* of human acts when we ask which acts would be rational not in this or that respect but *simply speaking*—what kind of activity is good for a human being not in this or that respect, but simply as a human being. But that consideration is for later.

Now given that you have an aim, an intention, to have a drink, it follows that you want to do something about it—for instance, go into a pub or an off-licence or the house of a generous friend. When you recognize some action, some means by which you may expect to gain what you intend, then,

Aquinas argues, you want this means, precisely as means, with the same desire with which you want the end.

Now sometimes it is perfectly obvious what means you should take to achieve your end. If you are crossing a street and your aim is to avoid being flattened by the bus you suddenly see bearing down on you, you will, without thinking a great deal about the matter, jump out of its way. Here you have a decision which is not merely instinctive but which has not needed any of what Aquinas calls 'deliberation'; you do not weigh up various courses of action you might take before choosing one of them, but nonetheless you make a rational decision.

Now if there is any deliberation to be done it must of course take place *before* you make a decision, and so it is a little strange to find that in the *Summa* Aquinas treats of decision first, at Prima Secundae, question 13, and then *after* that treats of deliberation in questions 14 and 15. This has puzzled people quite a lot. But I think it is simply because decision, *electio*, is *essential* to any rational human action, whereas deliberation is not always important, and often doesn't occur at all. Aquinas points this out:

> Deliberation is a kind of inquiry *(inquisitio)*. Now we are wont to inquire into things we are doubtful about ... There are two factors in a situation which put elements of human activity beyond doubt. First, when determinate ends are reached along determinate ways, as in skills that are governed by fixed rules ... a calligrapher does not question the shape of the letters of the alphabet; his skill takes this for granted. Second, when it is a matter of little moment whether a thing is done in this way or that ... Here then, as Aristotle notices, there are two matters which, although they conduce to an end, we do not deliberate about, namely trifles and those produced by well-established methods.[2]

---

[2] *Summa Theologiae*, 1a2ae, 14, 4.

I labour this point a bit because Aristotle also said something that came down to the Latin West as: 'Choice [decision] is desire of what has already been deliberated on', which might seem to make deliberation essential to true decision.

I am sure it must seem pedantic to worry about such matters, but in fact it is of great importance. The idea that deliberation (*consilium*) is what makes human acts human, rather than decision (which, in fact, may not need deliberation at all) may be a crucial mistake. I think that for the most part thinking about morality in recent centuries has sharply divided the work of reason seen as deliberation from the operation of the will seen as decision. Reason, it has been thought, may provide us with the correct moral rules: what it is proper to do or not to do in certain circumstances. You may come to be fairly expert about this or at any rate feel pretty confident that you have it about right. Of course since everyone from Aristotle onwards has insisted that human action takes place in particular concrete circumstances, you cannot be scientifically certain about what ought to be done (it is usually easier to be sure about what ought *not* to be done), and this concreteness, complexity and particularity is where the skill in *casuistry* comes in. Anyway, right or wrong, this is the best determination you can come to about what is to be done. This is the verdict of your conscience.

However, there then remains (for this way of thinking) the decision as to whether you will follow your conscientious verdict or not. You are *intellectually* as clear as can be expected about the right thing to do, but whether or not you will do it is another matter. And this is what is decided by will, 'free will'. The 'free' in 'free will' seems to mean that its operation must be quite unpredictable. It just arises from some impenetrable depth within you, and there is no way of predicting what its verdict will be.

I hope I have succeeded in making clear the difference between Aquinas's account, in which your will, your being attracted, is involved from the very beginning and as an element in your practical thinking, and the view that you can have a rational and clear vision of the morality of the matter but still need an appeal to the 'free will' to make the link with reality, with what you are going to do. Of course Aquinas knew perfectly well that you can usefully think about moral issues in which you are not personally engaged (other people's problems for instance). What he does not have is a theory in which you can treat yourself as another person and then, at the end, add a little touch of practicality and personal relevance by way of the will.

Chapter 10

Deliberative Reasoning

I was suggesting at the end of the previous chapter that when, as frequently happens, the human decision to act, *electio*, is preceded by *consilium*, deliberation, both of these are the work of human reason and concomitantly of the will (the human capacity to be attracted by what is thought to be good). I also suggested that each involves a different kind of human reasoning: deliberation is reasoning about what means will achieve the end I have in view; decision is about whether I (being who I am) will take these means to the end. To simplify the matter (perhaps to oversimplify it), deliberation is about possible means to my *end*; decision is about whether *I* shall take these means.

When Aristotle discusses human action he presents it, as does Aquinas, as the action of a reasoning animal, and he presents it as a sort of syllogism which instead of concluding in a truth concludes in an action. Aristotle has puzzled his commentators by *sometimes* setting out such syllogizing with a proposition like 'I want to be cured', followed by 'This medicine will cure me' etc., and *sometimes* beginning with a proposition like 'Sons should respect their fathers' followed by 'I am a son so ...' etc. I want to suggest that the first of these represents typical reasoning about the suitability of means to an *end*, while the second represents typical reasoning about the suitability of means to the *agent*. Let us first look briefly at deliberative reasoning (about means and ends).

The first thing to notice here is the difference between this kind of *inquisitio* or enquiry into means, and a syllogism in *theoretical* reasoning.

In writing the *Prior Analytics* Aristotle was inventing logic in the modern sense, what we have come to call 'symbolic logic'. With the use of letters of the alphabet to indicate variables he sets out patterns of necessary implication, like this, for example:

> If A is predicated of all B,
> and B is predicated of all C,
> then, necessarily, A is predicated of all C.[1]

Notice that the variables A, B, and C all signify classes of things, not individuals, and notice that the implication takes the form of 'if ... then ...'. An illustration of such a pattern of necessary implication might be this. Suppose for A we write '(being) mortal' and for B write 'being human beings' and for C write 'Greeks'. Then we would get:

> *If* being mortal is predicated of all human beings,
> and *if* being human beings is predicated of all Greeks,
> *then*, necessarily, being mortal is predicated of all Greeks.

Notice in passing how this sophisticated account of a pattern of implication became corrupted, during the logical Dark Ages of post-Renaissance writing, into what was imagined to be an Aristotelian syllogism: 'All men are mortal; Socrates is a man; therefore Socrates is mortal.' This does not display an 'if ... then ...' form. Its premisses are indicative sentences and the 'therefore' indicates that this is not a pattern of implication but an actual argument, and the 'Socrates' shows that it seeks to be not about a class of things but about an individual (which for any Aristotelian, unlike a class of things, cannot be grasped by

---

[1] Aristotle, *Prior Analytics*, 25b37–40.

the intellect alone without bodily sensual contact of some kind).

But for Aristotle himself, logic is not a matter of arguments about men and mortality and Socrates but an account of purely intellectual patterns of necessary implication.

I say all this not to contrast real Aristotelian syllogistic with the debased 'logic' of the seventeenth and eighteenth centuries, but to contrast the patterns of implication that belong to theoretical, scientific reasoning with the patterns that belong to deliberative *inquisitio*.

In his book *Will, Freedom, and Power* Anthony Kenny points to two fundamental differences between these two patterns.[2] The first is that deliberative reasoning does not come to a *necessary* conclusion in the way that theoretical argument following a pattern of necessary implication does. Consider this argument:

> It is desirable to go to London,
> and if I board this train I will get to London,
> so it is desirable to board this train.

This reasoning shows not that I *have to* board this train, for there may be cheaper and more convenient ways of getting to London; but at least it is a *possible* means. In order to achieve the desirable aim of getting to London it will not be *necessary* but *sufficient* to take this train.

Kenny's way of putting it is that while theoretical reasoning is 'truth-preserving', practical reasoning of this kind is 'satisfactoriness-preserving'. What he means by this is that if you follow the patterns of necessary implication and start with true premises, you will not get a false conclusion—the truth of the premises will be preserved in the conclusion. In good practical reasoning, however, it is the satisfactoriness of the

---

[2] Anthony Kenny, *Will, Freedom, and Power* (Oxford: Basil Blackwell, 1975), ch. 5.

premiss which is preserved (up to a point) in the conclusion. If getting to London is satisfactory (or desirable) then getting on the train will (up to this point) also be satisfactory (or desirable).

Another important difference, however, that Kenny notes between theoretical and practical reasoning is that a valid theoretical syllogism closes the matter and is unaffected by adding additional premisses to it; extra information is simply irrelevant. For consider:

> If all human beings are mortal,
> and all Greeks are human beings,
> then, necessarily, all Greeks are mortal.

This argument remains valid however much extra information you add to, say, the first premiss. If all human beings are mortal and there is an outbreak of plague in Nicaragua and my aunt thinks I am a heroin addict ... and so on, then necessarily if all Greeks are human beings, they are mortal. Regardless.

Things are very different, though, with the deliberative *inquisitio*, the search for suitable means. If we add further information to the premisses of such a syllogism we might get:

> It is desirable to get to London,
> and if I board this train it will get me to London, but it will be delayed for three days
> by leaves on the line and/or the wrong kind of snow, and in any case I
> wouldn't get a seat because it is packed with tourists from Carcassonne,
> Ozark, Alabama and so on ...

Such additions may make a considerable difference to the conclusion

> It is desirable to board this train.

In fact deliberation consists largely of looking around for *relevant* extra information, and this is one of the capacities to be found in the disposition we call the virtue of *phronesis* or *prudentia* or practical wisdom: to have an eye for relevant extra considerations; and practical wisdom (what Jane Austen calls 'good sense') is not a purely intellectual matter but is acquired by experience and involves memory and sensitivity to the concrete details of human living.

Let us now turn to decision itself.

In decision you take what seems, by deliberation or otherwise, to be efficient means (in relation to what they can achieve) and look at them in terms of their relation to the sort of person you, the agent, are. Decisive action arises from the recognition that *It is in me to do this*: 'This action is an expression of what I am and want.' The conclusion of decisive reasoning is not a proposition but an action or attempted action, and actions are not written on paper but performed, though they can be expressed on paper by a sentence in the imperative mood, e.g. 'Take this train.' This imperative is the rational command to yourself to do something. Of course, not everything you try to do gets done. You may decide to board the train and seek to do so but be pushed off by inebriated football fans. This does not show that you were not engaged in decisive activity, but simply that you are not omnipotent.

Decisive action, then, is not just any choice or whim but is, says Aristotle, the product of a certain *character*, a 'settled personality' as we might say nowadays. For Aristotle and Aquinas this is a matter of what dispositions you have acquired by education (or, for Aquinas, which have been infused in you by the presence in you of the Holy Spirit). Decisions can only be taken, in the fullest sense, by grown-ups. As you will have noticed, it is characteristic of this way of speaking of human action and evaluating it that, unlike the morality of the handbooks of 'moral theology', it is not simply concerned to say this action would be wrong (breaks a rule) and this other would be right (conforms to a rule) but is more centrally

91

concerned with education. (For Aquinas the outpouring of the Holy Spirit, which he also calls the 'New Law', is a form of divine education.) Education is learning how to be the kind of person who acts well by a kind of second nature; as you are educated you just naturally leave behind infantile greed and aggression and grow up to be someone who simply does not want to *be* like that. But that is not quite true for our present purposes. For we must think of being 'educated' into vice as well as into virtue; your settled personality may be one focused on, say, self-indulgence or 'intemperateness' and, if so, it will seem the obvious thing to do to seek every pleasure available regardless of most other considerations. A truly vicious person sees nothing wrong with what he does and is sceptical about people who claim to have a different scale of values. (Think of Thrasymachus at the beginning of Plato's *Republic*.) Anyway he is grown-up and decisive in his vice, just as the temperate or just person is grown-up in virtue; both are capable of full decisions that express what or who they are. Both of them stand in contrast to the immature, who have not yet acquired a settled character. Aquinas divides the immature into the *controlled* and the *uncontrolled*—in Latin, the *continens* and the *incontinens*. This is because in Aristotle, and classically, the discussion of them takes place in the context of sexual morality. We'll be looking at that important discussion in a moment.

You might put it this way. In the early stages of education a child, with luck, behaves well because she wants to please her parents or teachers or whatever. He or she is 'controlled' from outside. Her good acts do not spring immediately from herself, from what *she* is disposed to do, but for good but extraneous reasons. Her good act is done for a good reason—but it is not *her* good reason. If she has good parents and/or teachers she will learn to internalize her reasons and become, not just one who does the good thing, but a good person, who simply wants to do what is good and does it by her own decision, *of herself*. Now it is important to see that an almost exactly similar psychological process can take place with, say, a young Nazi brought up in the Hitler Youth to despise human beings of the 'wrong' race. You can be grown-up and decisive in vice as you can in virtue. A decision does not mean a good decision, but one that is fully *yours*.

So a young child may demand something by a simple whim. And no matter how stubbornly and vociferously he demands it he is not being decisive. This is often because his disposition is not in fact centred on what it purports to be but on, say, winning or losing a contest with his parents. Quite often if he gets what he demands he will lose interest in it.

One reason why I am deeply suspicious of the market economy, allegedly based on absolute freedom of choice, is that it seems to have no way of distinguishing between decisive choice and whim, and no analysis at all of adult human action. As I see it, adult decision is in important respects sacred; whim is not.

So, to put all this into a diagram:

	Good	Bad
Pre-adult state	Controlled (*continens*)	Uncontrolled (*incontinens*)
Adult state	Virtuous	Vicious

Now let us look at the problem set by Socrates concerning *akrasia* — (moral) weakness (sometimes called 'weakness of will', but erroneously).[3]

Socrates believed that it was not possible to do what you clearly knew to be bad, so, since manifestly people often do what is bad, he attributed this to their ignorance of the good. In his time the notion of will had not been developed in the way that it came to be with Augustine. Later, post-

---

[3] As discussed by Aristotle in *Nicomachean Ethics*, 7, 2.

Augustinian thinkers argued that we could avoid Socrates's position by saying that the spring of action is not knowledge but will and that, even after coming to a rational understanding of what is good for us to do, there is still required an independent decision of the will to do it or not to do it. These people made a sharp distinction between the contribution of the intellect in providing information as to the moral state of affairs (frequently as to the legal position—what obligations or rules am I under?) and the contribution of the will in moving me to action.

This position is not open to Aquinas, for whom the will is simply our being attracted by the good as it appears to our minds. The will is the 'being-attracted' component of practical knowledge. Nonetheless he does not take up a Socratic line. He does agree with Socrates that bad actions in one sense stem from ignorance, but for him it is not only true that will depends on understanding; it is also true that understanding depends on will. We come to know what we *try* to, or are *willing* to, find out; and when we have found things out we *consider* (put in the forefront of our minds) what we want to consider. We may, instead of considering what we rationally know to be the case, find it pleasanter to be doing something else. Aquinas takes from Aristotle an illustration from the different kinds of decisions that might be made about bad sexual behaviour, the decisions respectively of the temperate, the intemperate, the controlled, and the uncontrolled person.

In this case Aquinas's position is that what makes it possible for us to do what we know to be bad is not weakness of *will* but a sidelining of reason through *weakness* of *temperateness* or *strength* of uncontrolled *passion*. It will be clear from what we have already seen that a temperate person is not simply someone who on some occasion elects to act as a temperate person would act; she or he is one to whom it is 'second nature' so to act. Her emotional appetites are rationally integrated into the whole pattern of her *self*, so that her sexual desires, like her desires for drink or food or prayer, arise in an appropriate context. She is not at the mercy of such appetites in isolation but they contribute in their various ways to the harmony of her enjoyment of life and the enrichment of her life story. For Aquinas as, I suppose, for most people, the appropriate context of sexual relations is more complex than a simple delightful generative or quasi-generative act, a spasm of sexual pleasure. It involves both personal and social relationships and factors like faithfulness and commitment. We now know, as he did not, I think, that this is just as true of many fairly complex animals as part of their genetic inheritance. But in our case, because our lives and our community are crucially dependent on language and concepts, this complexity is something grasped by reason, and not simply an instinct.

So while other animals might simply find it *unattractive* to engage in sex outside its appropriate context, the human animal, in Aquinas's view, might find it *unreasonable* (but is also notoriously capable of finding it inappropriately attractive). The temperate person is one who is reasonable and organized in these matters and so sexual relations divorced from their context naturally seem to her inappropriate and distasteful, and just not *her*.

And so her decision is like this, as Aquinas explains in *De Malo* (note that Aquinas does not mean that every such decision is conducted by going through a piece of syllogistic reasoning, but only that the intellectual structure of the decision can be exhibited in this way):

Since any act, whether sinful or virtuous, comes from decision (*electio*), which is a deliberated desire, for deliberation is a kind of enquiry, it follows that in every act, good or bad, there is, as it were, an argument in syllogistic form. But the temperate person syllogizes one way, the intemperate (self-indulgent) another; and the controlled person (*continens*) one way, the uncontrolled (*incontinens*) another.

The temperate person is moved only in accordance

with the judgement (*iudicium*) of reason, and hence uses a syllogism of three propositions, as though arguing:

No fornication is to be committed.

This act is fornication.

So it is not to be done.

The intemperate, wholly given over to pleasure, also uses a syllogism of three propositions, as though arguing:

Everything delightful is to be enjoyed.

This act is delightful.

So it is to be enjoyed.

But both the controlled and the uncontrolled are moved in two ways; in accordance with reason they are moved to avoid sin, but sensual desire prompts them to commit it. In the controlled person the judgement of reason prevails, in the uncontrolled the promptings of sensual desire. Each therefore uses four propositions though they arrive at opposite conclusions.

The controlled person syllogizes thus: 1. No sin is to be committed (this he proposes in accordance with the judgement of reason); but in accordance with the prompting of sensual desire he also turns over in his mind the thought that: 2. Everything delightful is to be done. But because in him the judgement of reason prevails, his argument concludes under premiss 1. Thus: This is sinful, so this is not to be done.

The uncontrolled person, however, in whom the promptings of sensual desire prevail, starts from premiss 2 and concludes thus: This is delightful, so it is to be pursued.

Of such an uncontrolled person we can say that he sins through weakness. Although he knows in the abstract (*in universali*) what is to be done he does not consider it in the particular case before him; for he does not argue in accordance with reason but in accordance with sensual desire.[4]

---

[4] *De Malo*, 3, 9 ad 7.

If I am right in my view that the consideration of means, perhaps by deliberation (*consilium*), culminates in a decision (*electio*) evoked by relating the proposed course of action not directly to the *end* to be achieved, but to the *agent* who has this end, then the role of the first premiss that Aquinas quotes, 'No fornication is to be committed', is not to state a *rule* or *law*, but to express the *self* of the agent. It is simply because we are here concerned with the goodness or badness of decisions that this takes the form of a precept. The 'imperative mood' is, in many ways, a good expression of what we want. But what makes it a decision is not that it takes account of a precept (as I think Kant might say) but that it expresses the disposition, the formed stable character, of the agent, in this case her virtue of temperateness. So the first premiss might equally have been written 'I am no fornicator' and similarly, the conclusion, which is not a proposition but an action or attempted action, could be, instead of 'So it is not to be done', 'So I am not going to do it'.

The point Aquinas is specially wanting to make here is that it is relatively easy to understand the rationality (intellectual component) of the decision of the *virtuous* (in this case temperate) person. She may be subtle and sophisticated, but her decision is uncomplicated; she just does what comes naturally (or 'second-naturally') to her. Things are equally straightforward for the opposite character, the self-indulgent or intemperate person, who again is not just someone who acts intemperately on some occasion, like getting drunk, but someone who has a stable character and clear lifestyle: his overriding intention is to have as much pleasure as possible. A self-indulgent, intemperate person does not need to have further *reasons* for wanting pleasure, just as a virtuous person does not need further reasons for being chaste. So the intemperate person thinks as though reasoning like this:

> Everything delightful is to be enjoyed (that is, I am such a
> *self*, such a person, as desires in terms of pleasure, a self-
> indulgent person),

This act is delightful also,
So it is to be enjoyed (or: So I am naturally (or 'second-
naturally') enjoying it).

Each of these two, then (the temperate and intemperate
person), has a pattern of behaviour, and their behaviour is
more or less predictable, not because they are automatic and
unfree but because they have each become people in charge of
their own behaviour, with a clear and characteristic purpose,
not to be swayed by chance circumstances.

When we turn to the controlled and the uncontrolled person
(and here the same person may be either at different times)
things are a bit more complicated.

The person represented here is one who is immature in
virtue, who knows in theory what is reasonable, and thus good,
behaviour and would like to be reasonable, but has not, so to
say, interiorized this understanding. He does not have it as a
feature of his 'second nature' or an immediate spring of his
behaviour. His moral understanding plays the same role as Mr
Knightley does for the eponymous heroine of Jane Austen's
Emma: a 'super-ego', an external norm of reasonableness not
yet integrated into Emma's self. She also has an external norm
of unreasonableness in her father, Mr Woodhouse, that is also
not yet integrated into herself. This happens only after her
marriage, when Mr Knightley comes to live in *her* house,
together with the unconscious and irrational forces (the 'id')
represented by her immoral and undisciplined father.

So for this person (whether controlled or uncontrolled) the
recognition that fornication is bad is part of theoretical reason
rather than practical reason, a general proposition rather than
an immediate source of action. This person, lacking the virtue
of temperateness, also has unintegrated sexual desires, though
since he also lacks the vice of intemperateness (self-indulgence), these are not the mainspring of his lifestyle; he is
merely liable on occasion to make them the first premiss, as it
were, of his decision and action.

So, says Aquinas, there is the possibility of two premisses from which to begin. Either *No sin is to be committed* or (as with the intemperate man) *Everything delightful is to be enjoyed.* The controlled man starts from the first; the uncontrolled man (who may be the same person on another occasion) starts from the second.

I do not think that too much weight need be put on this, but I find it interesting that in Aquinas's text the *uncontrolled* and the *intemperate* man have virtually identical starting points to bring them to the same conclusion: *omne delectabili est prosquendum* (everything delightful is to be pursued) and *omni delectabili est fruendum* (everything delightful is to be enjoyed); whereas the *controlled man* and the *temperate man* conclude to the same action from *different* starting points. The temperate person has the starting point *nulla fornicatio est committenda* (no fornication is to be done) while the controlled person has *nullum peccatum est faciendum* (no sin is to be committed). The *virtuous* man has, as the object of his virtue, sexuality (as integrated into a pattern and a life story); his morality is a matter of his engagement with the concrete particulars of his story. The controlled man on the other hand has to fall back on a relatively abstract and general principle that sin is not to be committed. The temperate man, like the *in*temperate man, has an attitude to *sex*; the controlled man has only an attitude to *morality*. The first two, the temperate and the self-indulgent, in their opposite ways act immediately from themselves, engaging with these circumstances. The merely controlled man (acting from a sense of duty) is to some extent play-acting. No such difference is in question with regard to the intemperate and the *un*controlled; for the temptation of the uncontrolled, moved by simple sensual desire, is to adopt on *this* occasion exactly the premiss which the intemperate man accepts as a character, *all the time* and as a lifestyle.

So the intemperate, self-indulgent man sins through strength, through being himself, though, of course, a limited, warped, and distorted self; but the uncontrolled sins through weakness, through failing to be the kind of self he would like to be.

Chapter 11

Prudentia

Both the controlled and the uncontrolled do know what is good and what is bad in any given case; but, of course, knowledge, whether theoretical or practical, can be, and normally is, rather latent and dormant than in use. You knew during the last five minutes the capital of the US and the temperature of boiling water (as a matter of theoretical reason) and you knew how to tie your shoelace (as a matter of practical reason). If you were asked for the information or asked to tie your laces this knowledge would have been brought into play. But until then it was dormant. The controlled man *is*, and the uncontrolled is *not*, bringing into play a knowledge concerning good and bad. The uncontrolled man, if he had asked himself, could have made the sinfulness of his proposed action the spring of his behaviour. But he didn't ask himself: the attractive delights of sex or whatever won the day against the reasonable, grown-up considerations that come from understanding.

So, according to St Thomas's account, strength of passion *may* be allowed to exclude considerations of what is known to reason, or again it may not. *Akrasia* in Greek means lack of power, but the *kratesis* (power) in question that is lacking in the case of the uncontrolled man is, at least in Aquinas's interpretation, the virtue of temperateness, which is a reasonableness in the *emotional* life ordering it in relation to other aspects of life. What is not in question for Aquinas (nor, indeed, for Aristotle) is 'weakness of will', which at least until fairly recently has been the conventional rendering of *akrasia*.

That conventional view depends, of course, on the idea that there is a purely intellectual operation which can be carried out without any actual involvement in making a decision and can be done in your study, composing handbooks of 'moral theology', say, which delineate as accurately as possible the rules bearing on this or that case; and then there is something else which is an operation of will in the one who actually has to decide, a will which may or may not be strong enough to obey these rules. It is not difficult to see here the influence of the absolute distinction instituted by Kant between fact and value, but we may ask (and competent historians may perhaps tell us) whether there is a Kantian influence on moral theology or whether it is the other way round, that the division of fact and value has its roots in a theological tradition and found its way from there to Kant.

How you stand as between St Thomas and what I have called the conventional view has the most profound effect on what you think moral theology is and how you see moral education. In the Catholic Church moral education has been conceived for some centuries in a thoroughly legalist form of the conventional way: 'These are the rules and you must train yourself to obey or take the consequences.' All this produces David Lodge's typical Catholic question of the 1950s, 'How far can you go?' In the 1960s during the Second Vatican Council it was thought by some that such legalism had some connection with Thomas Aquinas, and this historical error was not wholly due, as you might naturally think, to sheer brute ignorance—though, of course, that was involved. The fact is that St Thomas has been fairly comprehensively misunderstood by his own disciples. The study of St Thomas was revived by the great Pope Leo XIII essentially as an intellectual answer to the mindset of liberal capitalism, which he thought of as the major contemporary threat to the gospel—whether in the social sphere, with the worship of the ruthless free market and the elimination of friendship as a basic social value, or in the increasing dominance of moral relativism in the culture of Europe. Aquinas having been co-opted into this campaign it is not too surprising that there grew up legalist and essentially voluntarist interpretations of Thomas (always called 'Thomism') which really did merit the strictures of many at Vatican II—this in spite of the fact that for at least two decades before that the Dominicans, especially in France, but also (heavily under the influence of the French) in England (here I am thinking especially of Gerald Vann, Thomas Gilby, and, above all, Victor White), rediscovered the authentic doctrine of Thomas, in which what was central was not *rules* or *natural law* but the virtue of *prudentia*—and not just the human virtue of *prudentia*, but a sharing in divine *providentia* by which we are guided in the life of *caritas* (sharing in divine love).

We still have a long way to go, however, in rehabilitating virtue and thus *prudentia* as the centre of moral thinking. The modern campaign in favour of virtue-based ethics, although it began in the 1950s, in Oxford, with the work of a tiny minority of people like Philippa Foot and Elizabeth Anscombe, was given its greatest international boost by Alasdair MacIntyre in *After Virtue*. There he identified the last gasp of Aristotelian virtue ethics and its death in the eighteenth-century idea that virtue was simply what made you keep the rules, the rules being what essentially defined human goodness. If you think this you do not in fact have a virtue-based ethics. Aquinas did.

So let's begin to look at *prudentia*—practical wisdom, good sense.

There are two major problems in talking about the virtue of *prudentia*. Well, actually there are two and a bit. So, let me first clear up the bit. This simply concerns the English translation or rather transliteration of *prudentia* into 'prudence'. In English culture the prudent person is the unromantic, canny person, to be contrasted with the free-spirited, large-souled person, willing to take risks, who 'doesn't count the cost' if something is worth doing, and so on. The prudent man is quintessentially the pragmatic businessman who always *does* count the cost. This is not at all what *prudentia* implies. To have the virtue of *prudentia* (it sounds better in Greek as *phronesis*) is indeed to be unromantic in the sense of avoiding some of the *vices* of romanticism: the 'prudent' person, for example, is not prepared to sacrifice truth for the sake of feeling. But at the same time he or she is fully aware of the slipperiness of truth in practice and the difficulty of being sure of it. Being prudent is in part a matter of being good at *consilium*—deliberation, the consideration of means with respect to ends—and the prudent person characteristically says, when a conclusion seems to have been reached: 'Yes, but don't we also have to take account of what would happen to Aunt Jemima if I did that?' To be prudent is often to *delay* a decision—on the traditional principle that deliberation should be slow and long, while action should be swift and decisive. And both of these belong to *prudentia*.

An exercise of *prudentia* culminates in *electio*, decision. The second and essential part of the exercise of *prudentia* is in answering the question 'Am I the sort of person who does this sort of thing?' And here one alternative to prudence is self-deception, posturing, play-acting on your private or public stage, and this I suppose is what a bad kind of romanticism often involves. *Prudentia* is not about a dry rationalism that ignores the complexities, especially the emotional complexities, of human decision and action. As pretty well every critic has said about Jane Austen's *Sense and Sensibility*, which is arguably the best treatise on *prudentia* in English, it is a mistake to make Elinor stand simply for *Sense* and Marianne for *Sensibility*. What is narrated is a subtle interaction and blending of the two.

Aquinas does not, in his treatment of *prudentia*, take any account of the English sense of 'prudence'; the vice he opposes to *prudentia* is *astutia*, a cunning which is a kind of bogus *prudentia*, the careful, rational pursuit of a *bad* end. He comes nearest to dealing with 'prudence' when he talks of the vices opposed to *magnificentia* and *magnanimitas*. But I think that is enough about the mean-minded modern English sense of 'prudence'.

Now to come back to the two *major* difficulties in talking of the virtue of *prudentia*. These are both rooted in the fact that *prudentia* is an *intellectual* virtue. It is opposed to at least a certain kind of stupidity. And many people would regard stupidity as more a misfortune than a vice. (What I have in mind is a kind of stubborn obtuseness.)

As I think I have suggested before, there is what we might call the Aristotelian level in Aquinas's thought, the level of what he talks of as the 'political virtues', meaning the virtues as defined by the *polis*. Here virtues are those dispositions which enable us to live together in society and thereby flourish—this society being based not upon justice and fairness but upon friendship, *philia*. Justice is essential to but derivative from friendship. But at a deeper level Aquinas is a thoroughgoing Augustinian and knows perfectly well that the earthly *polis*, however excellently developed, is only a shadow of the Kingdom, which again is not based upon justice but upon *agape*, *caritas*: friendship, indeed, but the friendship that God grants to us in his grace. I remind you of this because, at the Aristotelian level, Aquinas regards *prudentia* as the linchpin of the virtues, what holds them all together, and without which there is no true virtue.

Of course when he treats of the real depth of human living he insists that the foundation of it all is not any moral, or political, or human virtue at all but *caritas*, the divine friendship, the Holy Spirit that God graciously shares with us and enables us to share with each other. This *caritas* he calls the 'form', meaning the soul or life, of every virtue. As St Paul puts it, 'If I have not charity' then my courage, chastity, justice, friendship, and all the rest of it are sounding brass and clanging cymbals, all empty within. But having been given to share in the divine life, we then live it out in our human way and exercise not only our strictly and exclusively *divine* virtues of faith, hope, and charity but also our now divinized human virtues, and of these the central one is *prudentia*. Such is Aquinas's view and I think it is the essentially Catholic view as distinct from some Reformed views, especially those that play down the importance of moral virtue as a sort of deceptive substitute for grace, and reject any suggestion that 'grace perfects nature'.

But, as I say, there is a difficulty, especially in St Thomas's way of seeing it, in that at the centre of these divine/human virtues is what is not even a moral virtue but an *intellectual* one. We are first called upon, it seems, to be intelligent. Can this be true? This is the question that Aquinas looks at first in *Summa Theologiae* 1a2ae at question 56, article 3.

May I remind you of the rather curious structure of the Secunda Pars, which, after the Prima Pars has dealt with creatures coming forth from the hand of God, turns round and talks about the creature's (and mostly the human creature's) return to his source. The return of the human creature to God *can* be seen as the return of the sinner who has rejected God's grace but, by God's grace of forgiveness, returns to him. This is, I think, the major emphasis in Reformed theology. Grace is the remedy for *sin*. (And sometimes it seems as though, for the Reformers, human nature itself is a kind of sin.) The Catholic tradition is different. In this teaching the human creature does indeed need to return to God from sin, which involves being imperfectly human as well as wrenched away from divine life, and from this point of view grace is seen as healing. In this it coincides with some Reformed views—though not with some others, which cannot accept that we are yet really healed at all but only 'deemed' or treated by God as though we were healed. But, anyway, there is no disagreement between Catholics and Protestants that human beings, having been separated from God, are in need of his grace and can do nothing of themselves to deserve this grace, which, as the word suggests, is simply the *free* gift of God. Differences begin when

Catholics say that once we *have* received God's free forgiveness, we have begun to share in God's life and so there is a sense in which the good deeds we do through his grace are deserving of, for example, increased grace, and ultimately glory. Indeed, St Thomas's soteriology (his account of how we are saved by Christ) is centred on the idea that Christ, the human being, through the grace given him by the triune God, earned, merited, for *himself* his conquest of death *and*, for those who believed in him, their conquest of sin and death. For Aquinas it is Christ precisely as human and full of grace, a saint, who saves the human race.

But I mustn't get carried away by all this. What I wanted to say was that there *is* a return to God from *sin*, but Catholics hold that even if we had not sinned we would still be seeking a return to God, not this time because we are *sinners* but simply because we are God's *creatures*. For it belongs to the thing made that it should seek to reproduce, at least to *be like* its maker. Aquinas's model is what he calls the 'artist' and the thing he makes. As something is perfected by the work of the artist it becomes more and more like the idea of what it is meant to be that is in the mind of the artist. So the thing being made, seeking its own completion, its perfection, is necessarily seeking to conform with what is in the mind of the maker. Of course, what is in God is God. To seek what God has in mind for me is to seek God. This is part of Thomas's devout Augustinianism, something that Augustine himself developed from Neoplatonic thinking. The creature made cannot find rest except in returning to its maker; this indeed is how it finds its perfection.

Now all that was to explain the idea behind the Secunda Pars of the *Summa*: the return not just of the *sinner* but, more fundamentally, of the *creature* to God. The oddness of the structure is that Aquinas goes through the treatment twice. In the first part of the Secunda Pars (the *Prima Secundae*) he goes through it summarily and in general, and then in the second part (the *Secunda Secundae*) he treats in much greater detail how human beings return to God their maker and divinizer. It is all about how creatures (and not only creatures but actually sinful creatures) are brought back by God to himself. So the Secunda Secundae does not deal with questions about man's ultimate destiny, the psychology of human action (such as we have been discussing), the meaning of grace, and so on. All this it takes for granted, and devotes itself entirely to human virtues and vices: firstly those that concern all men and women, and then a short section at the end on the life of people called to a particular role in human history and the life of the Church (prophets, charismatics, religious life under vows). I think, by the way, that simply to look at the structure and content of the *Summa* is to find an excellent reason for reading Aquinas today, or any other day. But I mustn't get carried away.

So there is a brief treatment of *prudentia* in the first part of the Secunda Pars and a much more detailed examination of it, ten questions, in the second part. The treatment in the first part quickly deals with the very notion of an intellectual virtue. Good dispositions of our theoretical reason surely should be such things as sciences by which a man is a good chemist or biologist, but not thereby a good man—not, as Aquinas puts it, 'good *simpliciter*', good without qualification. That is what a moral virtue is. In this sense a virtue, a *moral* virtue, can only be a disposition of the will or, Aquinas adds, some power that is moved by the will. As usual he appeals once more to the interrelation of intellect and will in human practical life:

> The subject of a disposition (*habitus*) which is *simpliciter* called a virtue can only be the will or some other power in so far as it is moved by the will. The reason for this is that the will moves to their acts all those other powers that are in some way rational (as distinct from powers to digest or have dreams). That a man acts well is because he has a good will (*quod homo bene agat contingit ex hoc quod homo habet bonam voluntatem*).[1]

---

[1] *Summa Theologiae*, 1a2ae, 56, 3.

(This is as close as Aquinas ever gets to Kant, who said, 'Nothing is, in an unqualified sense, good except a good will.') Consequently, Aquinas goes on:

The virtue which actually makes him to act well, and not merely to be capable of doing so, must be either in the will itself, or in some power moved by the will. Now the intellect is moved by the will, as the other powers are; a man turns his mind to something because he wants to. Hence the intellect also, inasmuch as it is subordinate to the will, can be the seat of virtue in an unqualified sense. In this way the speculative [theoretical] intellect or reason is the seat of faith; for the intellect is moved by the command of the will to assent to what is of faith, since 'no man believes unless he is willing' [Augustine]. The practical intellect, on the other hand, is the seat of *prudentia*. Since this is right reason in doing [*recta ratio agibilium*—as distinct from skill, which is right reason in making something, *recta ratio factibilium, ars*] it is required [according to W. D. Hughes's translation] that a man be rightly disposed to the sources which justify this effective decision, that is to the ends of life. [What Aquinas is saying is that a man needs to be properly disposed in respect of the reasons for which he is acting, which are his aims: *ad principia huius rationis agendorum, quae sunt fines*.] And a man is well disposed in the matter of ends by rightness of the will [wanting to achieve good things] just as to the principles of theoretical truth he is disposed by the natural light of the creative mind (*intellectus agens*). Consequently, just as the subject of scientific knowledge is the theoretical intellect ordered by the light of the creative mind, so the subject of *prudentia* is the practical intellect ordered by a right will.[2]

---

[2] *Summa Theologiae*, 1a2ae, 56, 3. Here I am quoting, with modifications and a critical gloss, from W. D. Hughes's translation in vol. 23 of the Blackfriars edition of the *Summa Theologiae* (London: Eyre and Spottiswoode; New York, McGraw/Hill, 1969).

So, for Aquinas, the virtue of *prudentia*, by which, as with any virtue, a human being is made good in an unqualified sense (good at being human), is a disposition of the mind exercised on the *stage set* by a good will (that is, a will attracted by a good end, a good intention). *Prudentia* is not, for him, concerned with ends as such, but operates *in view of* whatever ends are willed to discover and decide upon what is to be done about the good end.

The second difficulty about seeing *prudentia* as an intellectual virtue is that the human intellect is not equipped to deal with concrete individuals but only with meanings, universal ideas. If I am right in interpreting Aquinas's account of understanding as the creation or discovery of a language in which our world can be interpreted, somewhat in the way in which we interpret the world sensually by the structure of our nervous system, then it is at least roughly right to say that the concepts in our minds are the meanings of the words we are able to use. Meanings of words of course are not individual things any more than the function of a hammer is an individual thing. Words may be used to refer to individual things, as a hammer may be used on an individual nail, but what they refer to is not their meaning. The meaning of a word is *how* it refers to things, not *what* it refers to. It is true that quite often we can save a lot of bother when explaining to someone the meaning of, say, the word 'oak tree' by pointing to one, but this presupposes a whole culture in which raising my arm and extending my forefinger urges someone to look in a certain direction, and presupposes that my interlocutor will not take 'oak tree' to mean the colour, location, or beauty of the tree. Pointing is simply part of the language which I would use in the hope of explaining the meaning of the word, which itself is simply the role of the word 'oak tree' in the English language.

When I say that understanding is the 'creation or discovery' of a language, I am referring to the fact that to learn a language (discover it) is just as creative in its way as to be the first inventor of a word. (I have been told that the verb 'to

Herbert' has or had some circulation in the city of Cork, brought there or created there by two young girls who stayed at Blackfriars, Oxford, with their parents once. It means to make a cup of tea with two teabags in the cup.)

Human action consists of individual actions at particular times in these or those circumstances, so *prudentia* must involve a grasp of the individual such as is impossible to the human intellect alone. You may say everything you know about, say, a person, you may give an account of her as long as you like, and yet your account could still apply in fact to someone else. You could, indeed, pick her out by indicating her relationship to another individual—'She is the only daughter of Mr Robinson'; but of course this presupposes that you can identify the individual Mr Robinson. You can in fact identify an individual only by calling on your sense-knowledge. You have met her, spoken with her, been in the same room with her, etc., etc. This means that the virtue of *prudentia*, although its subject is the intellect, also has to involve sense experience, sensitivity, memory, and indeed a sensitive evaluation of your experience. Aquinas argues that *prudentia* involves the senses, though not immediately the five external senses but what he calls the four 'interior senses'. Anthony Kenny is disparaging about these interior senses, doubting whether they are really senses at all, mainly because he thinks that senses are used for exploring the world around us.[3] I think he would get nearer to the truth if he began by recognizing that what makes something a *sense* is that it is a bodily activity by which we interpret the world. Aquinas speaks of external and internal senses in a quite literal way. Exterior senses are on the surface of our bodies, interior senses are inside, and (as we should say) at the meeting place of the whole nervous system, the brain. Aquinas had a great respect for the powers of sensation (and, incidentally, for the other animals who share them with us). A great deal of what post-Renaissance philosophers have attributed to the 'mind' as

---

[3] Anthony Kenny, *Aquinas on Mind* (London: Routledge, 1993), p. 39.

organizing our perceptions of the world is attributed by
Aquinas to the interior senses: thus he thought that other
animals had, as we have, a sensory power of evaluating the
world, and a sensory power of a certain kind of judgement.
Prudentia, thought Aquinas, brings these sensory powers into
play, and that is why, he says, it depends on experience and
develops through a long life, and, of course, can be impeded by
brain damage, as indeed can purely intellectual activity, which
in a different way also has to be accompanied by operations of
the interior senses.

For Aquinas, sensation is much more than the mechanical
reception of so-called 'sense-data' through eyes, skin, etc. Just
as our understanding of our world is our interpretation of it in
terms of the *historically developed* structure of language (what has
meaning has a role as part of some *structure*) so our animal
sensation is the bodily interpretation of our world in terms of
the *genetically received* structure of the nervous system. So besides
the five 'external' senses, he recognizes four 'interior' senses
(functions, we might say, of the brain) by which the input of
the external senses is worked up into what is sensually
meaningful for our bodily life. He writes (and here I just let
him speak for himself at some length):

> Since nature does not fail in what is needed, there have to
> be as many activities in the life of sensation as are
> sufficient for a truly functioning animal. And whatever of
> such activities cannot be reduced to a single source must
> be the work of different powers, since a vital power just is
> the immediate source of a vital operation.
>
> The life of a higher animal demands, however, not only
> that it perceive what is present here and now to the senses
> but also what is absent. Otherwise, since the behaviour of
> an animal follows upon perception, it would never be
> moved to seek what is absent; and this is clearly not the
> case with higher animals which move purposefully, in
> search of what is perceived to be absent. So such animals

need not only to receive the forms of sense objects while they are being affected by them but also to retain and preserve them.

Receiving and preserving must, however, involve different bodily operations, for moist areas receive an impression easily but preserve it badly, while with dry areas it is the other way round. Hence, since a sense power is exercised in the activity of a bodily organ, there has to be one power to receive sense forms and another to preserve them. Moreover, if an animal's behaviour were dependent simply on what it found sensibly attractive or disgusting we would not need to suppose it had any perception of things other than the reception of their forms, whether pleasing or displeasing. But an animal needs to approach or flee from what it encounters not only because its appearance is nice or nasty, but because it is either serviceable or dangerous. Thus, the sheep flees the wolf not because its appearance is unpleasant but because it is its natural enemy; and a bird collects straws not for the sake of their pleasant appearance but because they are needed for nest-building. So an animal has to perceive a meaning in things that is not the object of any external sense.

There has, then, to be a distinct bodily organ of this perception, since while the perception of sense forms is their affecting one of the senses, the perception of such *meaning* is not. So an animal's perception of sense forms involves both the particular external senses and also an interior, co-ordinating sense (*sensus communis*). Their retention and preservation requires *phantasmata* or, what is the same thing, *imagination*. For the imagination is a sort of storehouse of the forms the animal has sensibly received. An animal needs also a power of sensual evaluation (*sensus aestimativus*) by which it grasps a meaning that is not simply an object of an external sense. For the conservation of these it needs a *sense-memory* which stores up sense-meanings. An indication of this is that animals remember just what has meaning for them as, for example, dangerous or congenial. The sense of pastness which belongs to memory is another meaning of this kind. So far as sensible forms are concerned there is *no difference* between human and other animals: they are similarly the product of what affects the external senses. But when we come to the perception of sensual meanings there is a difference; for other animals perceive such meanings because they are naturally programmed so to do [instinctively] but the human animal does so by actively bringing the input of sense together.

So, what in other animals is called an innate [instinctive] evaluation, in humans is called 'cogitative'—finding such meanings by a process of comparison. It has also been called 'reason of particulars' (and is assigned by medical science a special organ in the middle of the head), for it compares *individual* sensual meanings as, in a parallel sort of way, the intellectual reason deals with and compares *universal* meanings. So far as memory is concerned, human animals do not just have sense-memory as their fellow-animals do—having a sudden recollection of past experience; they have a power of 'reminiscence', a quasi-reasoning search into the memory of past individual sense-meanings.[4]

---

[4] *Summa Theologiae*, 1a, 78, 4.

Chapter 12

Interior Senses I

I have been trying to explain the modern and medieval preference for talking about human behaviour in terms not just of individual actions and reactions but of powers, tendencies, dispositions and, in particular, of virtues and vices, rather than concentrating on episodic individual good or bad acts.

In Aquinas's view, central to this whole programme is some exploration of *prudentia* (*phronesis*), an *intellectual* virtue which is also essential to the *moral* virtues, which belong not first of all to intellect but to will and the other appetites. Aquinas's thesis is that *prudentia*, though a virtue of the mind, presupposes a certain (good) orientation of the appetites; but also this orientation of the appetites depends on a certain (true) assessment of the world, which is a matter of intelligence. The intellectual virtue of practical wisdom (*prudentia*) and the moral virtues of, say, justice, courage, or chastity have what biologists might call a symbiotic relationship; they feed off each other. So we should not put *knowing* what is rational and *wanting* to do it in quite separate compartments; they need each other. But generally speaking moral virtues will be primarily to do with what sort of things you aim at, your *ends*, while intellectual virtues will be to do with selecting and deciding on the *means* you will take to achieve them. The bad disposition of the practical intelligence which enables you to select the means to a bad end is *astutia*, the vice of cunning; the good disposition that enables you to decide well about what you will do about achieving a good end is *prudentia*, the virtue of practical wisdom. Now *prudentia*, though an intellectual virtue, has to deal with concrete individual situations, for all human actions are individual and unique. Purely intellectual skills cannot do this. No textbook of chemistry says anything about an individual grain of salt nestling amongst the millions of grains of sand on Miami Beach; instead it talks about the nature of salt, what sodium chloride is and its physical/chemical properties. No textbook of geometry tells you about the Louvre pyramid in Paris. Such books simply tell you about triangles and their mathematical properties. Textbooks of chemistry and geometry get their elegance and convincingness and necessity (so that when you understand what they say you exclaim, 'Yes, of course, I see it must be so') precisely by abstracting from individuals. We cope with individuals and, for example, distinguish one chemically identical grain of salt from another not by giving different accounts of them but, because we ourselves are individual bodies, they will have different physical relationships to our body: one grain is between my toes and the other in my hair. To refer to individuals as such we have to make use directly not of understanding but of the special kind of interpretation of the world provided not by language but by the structure of our bodies, by our nervous system: by sensation. For this reason an intellectual virtue like *prudentia*, which has to cope with individual human actions, has to be not only a disposition of the intellect but also of our sensibility.

This does *not* mean a disposition of our external senses—as we might make our sense of sight sharper by getting new glasses, or improve our hearing by getting the wax out of our ears. For practical wisdom we need not improved *external* senses but good dispositions of the *internal* senses; these are the *sensus communis* (or 'co-ordinating' sense), the *imaginatio* (retaining what it was like to experience something), the *sensus aestimativus* (or 'evaluating' sense, which grasps the sensual significance of bits of experience), and the sense-memory (which stores up what it was like to have such significant experiences).

To be right about *prudentia*, then, we need to consider our interior-sense knowledge as well as what we know purely intellectually. And that is why I am talking about interior senses now.

Aquinas begins his brief account of the interior senses[1] with 'Nature does not fail in what is needed.' It would have been altogether in tune with this thinking if he had said, 'Nature does not hesitate to fail in what is *not* needed,' which is sort of the basis of the Darwinian principle of natural selection. For both Aquinas and Darwin you give an intelligible account, an explanation, a *ratio* of the structure, powers, and behaviour of animals when you see them in the perspective of survival, not just of an individual but of a whole species. Aquinas, of course, had no notion of the evolution of species and was content to think of them, as we still are content to think of hydrogen, as dating from near the beginning and remaining unchanged. He would I am sure have been delighted by the sheer simplicity and beauty of the idea that when the habitat of a species changes, those members which by good luck have heritable (genetically determinable) features which enable them to cope with the new situation will live longer and have time to breed more progeny with the same genetic advantage over less fortunate ones, so that gradually those that inherit the useful feature will constitute the only surviving form of the species. In accordance with his principle that we do no honour to the Creator by belittling the power and perfections of his creatures he would of course have seen this process of *nature explaining itself* as a typical manifestation of the wisdom of the Creator. Aquinas never saw God and nature as rivals (not even God and human nature). Where he does explicitly teach something incompatible with the thought of some (but not by any means all) Darwinians is in his puzzle about the origins of the human

---

[1] *Summa Theologiae*, 1a, 78, 4.

capacity to understand. He cannot see how this could be caused by powers within nature or even how it could be inherited, because he thought that understanding was a power to transcend matter and individuality, and so he teaches that each human soul is the product of a new and separate act of creation by God. (Following a mistaken bit of Aristotelian biology he thought that this creative act of God took place forty days after the conception of the embryo—except, interestingly, in the case of Jesus, who was human and divine from the moment of his conception.) This disagreement of Aquinas with most Darwinians about the alleged evolution of intelligence becomes less sharp when we realize that we *still* have the same puzzle about the origins of understanding that Aquinas had. No one has yet, to my knowledge, provided a coherent and satisfactory evolutionary account of the origins of language. Plenty of stuff is known about its *development* once there, but not about the origins, and anyway the development of language takes place by *history* not by *evolution*. Meanwhile, to envisage each human being as a unique creation by God, comparable to the creation of the entire universe, and not simply and totally the product of her ancestors, seems to me a valuable barrier to any kind of totalitarianism—though, of course, that is no evidence that it is true.

Since I have been looking at questions that are asked both by Aquinas and by our own contemporaries in philosophy, I would like to turn, just for a moment, to a modern philosopher, an admirer of Aquinas as a philosopher, who shares Aquinas's puzzles about what in nature could bring about intelligence— as he (and I) would put it, the 'origin of human language'. So I wish to refer yet again to Anthony Kenny. Perhaps I ought to add a biographical note here. Dr Kenny is very definitely *ex*-Christian, a genuine agnostic who is profoundly sceptical (to say the least) about such notions as the immortality of the human soul. Nevertheless holding, as he does, very similar views to those of Aquinas about what it is to be a rational being (it means to be a linguistic animal) he shares Aquinas's puzzlement about how language fits into the natural causality of the world, and in particular into the process of natural selection. He writes:

Now the rule-governed nature of languages makes it difficult to explain the origin of language by natural selection. The explanation by natural selection of the origin of a feature in a population presupposes the occurrence of that feature in particular individuals of the population. Horses, for instance, may have developed the length of their legs through evolutionary stages. One can very easily understand how natural selection might favour a certain length of leg: if it were advantageous to have long legs, then the long-legged individuals in the population might outbreed the others. Clearly, where such explanation of the occurrence of features is most obviously apposite, it is perfectly possible to conceive the occurrence of the feature in single individuals. There is no problem about describing a single individual as having legs *n* metres long. (There may or may not be a problem about explaining the origin of the single long-legged specimen; but there is no logical difficulty in the very idea of such a favoured specimen.)

Now it does not seem at all plausible to suggest, in a precisely parallel way, that the human race may have begun to use language because the language-using individuals among the population were advantaged and so outbred the non-language-using individuals. This is not because it is difficult to see how spontaneous mutation could produce a language-using individual; it is because it is difficult to see how anyone could be a language-user at all before there was a community of language-users.

In writing this book I am using language, and that I am doing so depends no doubt on decisions of my own and is conditioned in all kinds of ways by the physiology of my own body. But whatever I did, whatever marks I made on paper or keys I tapped on a keyboard, they could not have the meaning my words now have were it not for the existence of conventions not of my making, and the activities of countless other users of English.

If we reflect on the social and conventional nature of language, we see something odd in the idea that language may have evolved because of the advantages possessed by language-users over non-language-users. It seems almost as odd as the idea that golf may have evolved because golf-players had an advantage over non-golf-players in the struggle for life, or that banks evolved because those born with a cheque-writing ability were better off than those born without it.

Of course, in fact, games like golf and institutions like banks were not evolved by natural selection: they were invented or developed through the voluntary choices of human beings. One could not explain the origin of language in the same way. In order to be able to invent an instrument for a particular purpose you need to be able to conceive the purpose in advance and devise the invention as a means of achieving the purpose. It is not possible that someone who did not have a language could first of all conceive a purpose that language could serve and then devise language as a means to serve it. Nor could language be hit upon by accident, as some human procedures were—as in the legend that pork was first roasted when somebody's house was burnt down with his pig inside. One cannot conceive of somebody's being the first person accidentally to follow a set of linguistic rules, as one can conceive of him being the first accidentally to set fire to his house.[2]

Dr Kenny's argument here seems to appeal to roughly the

---

[2] Anthony Kenny, *The Metaphysics of Mind* (Oxford: Clarendon Press, 1989), pp. 155–6.

same point that I was making in Chapter 7 starting from Wittgenstein's claim that there cannot be a private language. I argued then, if you remember, that meanings, the meanings of words, could never be my personal *property* in the way that my sensations and feelings are my property. It is true that since we belong to the same species and have approximately the same genetic and bodily structure it is very likely that your sensations are much the same as mine in similar situations. But you cannot have my sensations; you can only have your own, which are *your* private property. It is quite otherwise, however, with the meanings upon which language depends. These meanings, 'the rules for the use of these signs', are neither my property nor yours, they belong to no individual; they belong to the language.

Language thus depends on what transcends individuality, so that each one of us shares exactly the same meaning of the signs we use (unless, of course, we use them incorrectly—but that is something quite publicly detectable and has nothing to do with you having a secret private meaning in your head that is all your own). And, as I was also saying, to transcend individuality in this way is, in Aquinas's language, to be immaterial. That is why Aquinas thinks that to exercise our capacity for using language, our intelligence cannot be a bodily material process, but transcends materiality.

So the human animal has a *vital* activity (a part of our *living* or, as Aquinas puts it, an operation of the human *soul*) which is not a bodily process. And, just to pursue that thought a little more, this means that human life, the human soul, does not simply consist in the animation of an animal body, as does the life or soul of other, non-linguistic animals. The soul of this giraffe is nothing but what makes it a *living* material being. Its work is so to say exhausted in being the principle in virtue of which the giraffe is alive, and not a machine or the corpse of what used to be a giraffe. Every operation of the giraffe soul (every vital operation) is necessarily an operation of the giraffe's body. Now this is not the case with the human soul, one of whose operations (alongside being the life-principle because of which we see and digest our food and feel affection for or fear of bits of the world) is using symbols in terms of their meanings, which cannot itself be a bodily activity. No configuration or activity of my brain cells could be an idea or concept or meaning; any such configuration would be my private property distinct from yours, just as my toenails are distinct from yours. To the argument that you can interfere with somebody's ability to entertain meanings by damaging his body, especially his brain, Aquinas replies that this is because for us, at least in this life, understanding has always to be *accompanied by* some kind of bodily activity of the *imaginatio*, or as he often says, some *phantasmata*. This is most clearly the case when your thinking is accompanied by an imaginary conversation with yourself—imagining what it would be like to speak bodily; but it is also often the case that we think in pictures or with imaginary or constructed diagrams. But, in any case, Aquinas would and did (I think rightly) argue that thinking itself could not be any such operation of a sensitive bodily power (as we should say, an operation of the brain), which for him is what *imaginatio* is.

Because, as I have said, the meaning of a giraffe's soul is exhausted in being the physical, sensitive life of the giraffe, it follows that the idea of a giraffe's soul as having a subsistence of its own apart from the subsistence of the giraffe makes as much and as little sense as the Cheshire cat's grin having a subsistence distinct from that of the Cheshire cat, or the height of a building remaining when the building has been knocked down. But if the human soul has an operation of its own that is not in itself an operation of the human body, then it is not the same kind of nonsense to say that it has a subsistence of its own which does not have to be that of the body. This, thinks Aquinas, at least leaves open the possibility of what Aristotle would call 'some part of the human soul', the rational part, still subsisting after the corruption of the body. But Aquinas is clear that this would not be a case of me surviving beyond the grave. '*Anima mea non est ego*,'[3] he says flatly: 'My soul is not me.' Moreover there are deep puzzles about how such an independently subsisting soul could have *any* operations, even thinking, without any body to animate. Aquinas speculates bravely on how a 'separated soul', at least in heaven, could somehow think as well as have the understanding which is the beatific vision (which fortunately does not depend on human concepts but on the Word of God).[4] It is all rather an uphill struggle and it is with a sort of relief that Aquinas reminds us that in the Scriptures it is not immortality of soul that we are promised but the resurrection of the body and this means that the blessed will be themselves, body-animated-by-soul, to enjoy, besides the beatific vision, human communication with each other in whatever way the transfigured body (what Paul calls a 'spiritual body') makes possible.

But we have had rather a long set of footnotes; let us get back to Aquinas's account of the interior senses.

The five exterior senses through their bodily organs, of which the basic one is the skin, the organ of touch, *begin* the sensual interpretation of the world. But if we were simply left with these five separate sources of passivity to the world, our experience would be just as somebody (I think it was William James) said of a baby's initial experience: 'a big buzzing blooming confusion'. I do not of course think that this *is* a baby's experience, for sensing is not sensing that does not *interpret* the world, and I can think of no reason why a baby or, for that matter, an unborn foetus should have the organs of sense without them being in use to do that interpreting. Simultaneous with the operations of the exterior senses there must be a co-ordination of their input so that they provide some sensuous information. 'Information' is a valuable word, deriving as it does from the medieval sense of *forma* as *meaning*, *significance*, *interpretation*. What we experience, for Aquinas, is

---

[3] *Commentary on 1 Corinthians*, 15, 2.
[4] *Summa Theologiae*, 1a, 12.

not 'sense-data', e.g. the alleged red patches that, in the empiricist scheme of things, were supposed to be the primitive and pure inputs of the sense of sight, but what (since around 1912, anyway) we have come to call the gestalt. The marvellous and ingenious experiments and observations of three great German psychologists (Kohler, Koffka, and Wertheimer) on what apes perceived restored to the twentieth century the medieval notion of the *sensus communis*, the co-ordinating work of the brain. What was already suggested by Aristotle in the *De Anima*[5] that there has to be a bodily co-ordination and discrimination of the external senses, is taken up by Aquinas, who notes the connection between the sense of touch (as the basic sense) and the *sensus communis*: 'All the other senses are founded upon touch ... man is the most touch-perceptive of all animals and amongst humans those most sensitive to touch are the most intelligent. For sensitivity of skin goes with mental insight.'[6] And in his *Commentary on 'De Anima'* (601–2) Aquinas remarks:

Aristotle observes that whereas we are able to distinguish not only between black and white or sweet and bitter (by exterior senses), but also between white and sweet and indeed between any one sense object and another, it must be in virtue of some *sense* that we do this, for to know sense objects as such is a sensuous activity: the difference between white and sweet is for us not only a difference of ideas, which would pertain to the intellect, but precisely a difference between sense impressions, which pertains only to the sense faculty. If this be true, then the most likely sense-faculty would seem to be *touch*, the first sense, the root and ground, as it were, of the other senses, the one which entitles a living thing to be called sensitive ... but this discrimination cannot be attributed to touch

---

[5] Aristotle, *De Anima*, 3.
[6] *Summa Theologiae*, 1a, 76, 5.

precisely as a particular sense, but only as the common ground of the senses, as that which lies nearest the root of them all, the *sensus communis* itself.[7]

And then, leaping seven centuries, we come to John Lewis and Bernard Towers:

> The association of a very sensitive skin with the largest central nervous system ever produced in any animal group is by no means fortuitous. It is not only the epidermis that is developed from the embryonic ectoderm [the outer layer, or skin, of an embryo in the earliest stage] ... The brain and spinal cord, and all the nerves of the body are also derived from the same cells of the embryo ... In the course of evolution *Homo sapiens* has developed a remarkable brain ... He has also developed a remarkable skin, which constitutes the largest sense-organ of the human body. This is no chance affair. Human brain and human skin are not unrelated variables ... For all that our special sense-organs like eyes and ears are very important, it is true to say that skin is our basic and principal means of communication with the environment ... Skin has become, in man more than in any other animal, a vast receptor-organ for information from the environment. In so doing it has lost some of its ancient protective qualities, such as hard scales, coarse dense hair, and sheer thickness. But the gains have been immeasurably worth-while, because increased receptivity means increased awareness and freedom. We no longer need heavy biological armour-plating to stay alive, because our brains have made us smart enough to defend ourselves intelligently ...[8]

---

[7] *Commentary on De Anima*, 3, 3.
[8] John Lewis and Bernard Towers, *Naked Ape or Homo Sapiens?* (New York: Humanities Press, 1969), pp. 41ff.

What I have tried to illustrate with these quotations is the common interest of pre-Cartesians and post-Cartesians in the unity of sensibility. The input of the senses is not a set of separate sense-data but a harmonious pattern. I say 'harmonious' in order to avoid saying 'intelligible', for of course we are still in the world of the senses and it is most important that we are; we do not need the mind to make sense of sense. What we have to think of here is something like the perception of music, of musical rhythm and musical harmony. The senses are that by which we are *in tune* with our world. I find it fascinating that when Aquinas, following Aristotle, said that touch was the foundation of all the senses, he spoke better than he knew; it has taken twentieth-century evolutionary biology to spell out just exactly how the structures of the sense organ of touch (the skin) and the whole nervous system including the brain arise out of the skin (the 'ectoderm') of the embryo. The role of the *sensus communis* is to bring the diverse inputs of the five senses back to their original unified source, which brings them together and, therefore, distinguishes, discriminates them. It is only by bringing them back to their tactile source that this is possible.

In my view the *sensus communis* has another aspect: as the source of an animal's self-awareness. The *sensus communis*, because it presents the world not as a 'buzzing blooming confusion' but as harmonious objects over against us, is thereby the sensuous appreciation of the animal's identity. Remember that the *sensus communis* belongs to other animals besides ourselves. The cat and the coelacanth, if they could speak, would not make the error of saying 'I think, therefore I am' but 'I sense an objective world of things which are not me; therefore *I* am.' It is in this way that other animals (but also human linguistic animals) are aware of their identity—with a sensual self-awareness that is there before the linguistic animal gets going with her conceptual analysis of identity. These two functions of the *sensus communis*, (1) to discriminate and order the inputs of the external senses into a set of harmonious patterns, as objects, and (2) to provide a basis for the sense of identity over against the objects 'out there', are interestingly verified by a modern experience. People who have used the drug LSD report two strange effects. One is an interchange-ability of sensations. They say they seem to see sounds and hear colours and smell both. The other is that they have a sense of merging into the whole world around them, of unity with the universe. Now both these effects are exactly what you would expect from a suppression of the *sensus communis*: a collapse of ordered discrimination amongst the senses and a loss of the sensual awareness of one's separate identity. During the 1960s people like Timothy O'Leary and his followers found great religious or mystical significance in the disappearance of individual identity. For me the significance lay more in the confirmation that the body is not only, being material, the *metaphysical* basis for our individuation (unlike angels, we are many individuals of the same nature) but in its interior senses is the *psychological* basis of our awareness of individual identity. The religious bit can take care of itself.

Chapter 13

Interior Senses II

I have been talking about the importance for Aquinas of the 'co-ordinating sense' (*sensus communis*). Aquinas would not deny, so far as I know, that you might, exceptionally, have isolated input of one external sense: you might unexpectedly be overwhelmed by an appalling stench, or shaken by a very loud noise; but I think that he would conceive of these as incomplete experiences in that the intensity of one sensation had blotted out the inputs of other senses so that you were offered something more like a blow or a kick than a gestalt, and hence no sense knowledge, not a true bodily experience. It seems to me that, for Aquinas, receiving the forms of sense objects (the phrase is *species sensibilium*) means receiving information, the sensations derived from the external senses as processed by the *sensus communis*; it is the whole sense process, both in eye or nose and brain, that is in question, and this is the *receptive* function of the *sensus communis*. But, since we and many of our fellow-animals also seek what is not at present affecting us through the external senses, we need to *retain* and preserve the forms we have received in sense experience. And this role is accomplished by what Aquinas calls *imaginatio*: the storehouse of species, the forms sensually received, a sense of what it is like to experience sensually. He saw the *sensus communis* and *imaginatio* as needing two separate interior sense organs, since one should be good at receiving an impression (like softened wax or damp mud) and the other bad at receiving but good at retaining (like hardened wax or dry mud).

It is most important to notice the difference between Aquinas's *imaginatio* and the English word 'imagination'. In English, 'imagination' is an intellectual capacity, indeed perhaps the highest intellectual capacity we have: what enables us to (in Edward De Bono's phrase) think *laterally*. We speak of a 'leap of the imagination' when talking of the insight Newton had under his apple tree or Einstein in his lift. It is what genius is about. It is what distinguishes computers from great chess players. It is why there is no such thing as 'artificial intelligence'—because intelligence is not displayed in very fast calculation but in insight. Aquinas thought that the reasoning linguistic animal was the highest form of *material* life because it is able to reason but the lowest form of *intellectual* life because it needed to reason. Neither angels nor, of course, God needs to reason any more than they need to eat and drink; their intellectual lives are more like pure insight.

But let me explain that some more. Whenever you hear someone say: 'Well, it stands to reason, doesn't it?,' you are being given a warning sign to look rather carefully at the grounds for this assertion and work out whether in fact they function as reliable grounds for whatever it is they are supposed to be the reasons for, as in 'It stands to reason that a Nigerian is not going to be as good as a Frenchman at cooking French food.' When Aristotle invented logic by writing the *Prior Analytics* his aim was to stop people thinking that something 'stands to reason' when in fact no relevant reason had been provided. His aim was not to help people to make a lot of rational arguments, but to hinder them from making bogus arguments. He mapped out a schema of what would be valid implications not in order to encourage people to construct lots and lots of valid syllogisms but to stop them producing invalid ones. You may say, I think, that the better someone is at reasoning the fewer pieces of reasoning she accepts—rather as the better someone is at medicine the fewer quack remedies she believes in. Nevertheless the notion that human intelligence consists in making syllogisms is so deeply ensconced in our culture that we don't even notice it is there; it is taken for granted. This, I think, has something to do with the popularity of a cast of mind called 'rationalism' in the seventeenth and eighteenth centuries (indeed it stands to reason that this is so) and possibly the worst consequence of rationalism was the reaction it inevitably provoked. The Romantics, understandably unconvinced that human intelligence could be reduced to calculation, recommended abandoning reason in favour of feeling, emotion, and the 'reasons of the heart'. And all this confusion arose simply from people not recognizing that human intelligence, at its peak, is imaginative (in the modern sense of imagination) and that the valuable function supplied by logic is that of checking the validity of your insights. A business needs an annual audit but only chartered accountants are in the business of annual audits. If there were *only* chartered accountants there would be *no* chartered accountants.

Partly I am saying this to cast doubt on the idea that if you produce an artificial animal (all machines are simulated animals) which helps you to discover the end of a complex calculation with extraordinary speed (much much faster than if you used pencil and paper or talking either publicly or quietly to yourself) you have somehow produced a mechanical intelligence. What you have is what is metaphorically called a 'calculator' because it is of immense use to *you* when you calculate. A computer is intelligent in just the same way that a pencil or a piece of paper is intelligent. But partly, and more immediately, I am saying this in order to distinguish 'imagination' in the modern sense, which is almost synonymous with intelligence, from *imaginatio* in Aquinas's sense, which is of great interest but not the *same* interest.

Imaginatio is a sense power, and an operation of the brain. It is a myth that the brain is somehow the 'organ' of thought. I think, with Aristotle and Aquinas, that there is not and cannot be any organ of thought, for reasons I have suggested already. The brain is amongst other things the organ of the interior senses, the centre of the network of nerves which constitute the structure of the nervous system and give significance and actuality to sensation. What I mean by saying 'significance and actuality' is that sensation just is part of the operation of the nervous system (that is its *significance*) and that the nervous system is what makes it happen (that is its *actuality*), and in the higher forms of animal life, such as that of rats and ourselves, the brain is the centre of this bodily system. The brain, to say it just once more, could not be the organ of understanding meanings because meanings could not be private, material, individual things, like brains and their operations, but belong to language. And they do not exist in language in the way that the special sounds of words or shapes of letters exist in language as part of what it *materially is*; meanings exist in language as what it *expresses*.

Aquinas wants to say two things about *imaginatio* and understanding. *First*, he thinks that they are quite *distinct*. He says that it was the great achievement of Aristotle to make this clear (it was, in my view, the great anti-achievement of David Hume and the empiricists to confuse them again with all their talk of 'ideas' as faint copies of 'sense impressions'). But, *secondly*, they are *inseparable*. I think he is right about this, but I do not think that he gives a good account of why he is right. I mean I think he gives an excellent account of why thinking is not just a refined kind of sensing or *imaginatio*, why understanding cannot be any physical process; I do not think he gives so good an account of why understanding has to be accompanied by or associated with a physical process. I think it is possible to give a better account of this than does Aquinas, who though he says it must be so sometimes seems to talk as though it were merely a contingent empirical fact. This better account is based on making the shift that some modern interpreters of Aquinas make (I do not, of course, mean the neo-scholastics and so-called 'Thomists' of the early part of this century, but people like Peter Geach, David Burrell, Denys Turner, and Anthony Kenny), all of whom, in explaining the essential connection of thought and language, start from the language end instead of, as Aquinas does, starting from the thought end. Aquinas is quite clear that every thought we have can, in principle, be expressed in language; what he does not say is that human thought *has* to be the significance expressed by some bodily symbols because human thought just *is* the capacity to use language (in the broad sense of symbols used in accordance with conventional rules). Or, to put it another way: *we* analyse understanding and thinking in terms of human communication whereas *Aquinas* analyses communication in terms of understanding and thinking. This is no great matter, since we should all be non-Cartesians and clear about the vital connection between being a rational animal and being a linguistic animal. But I think the twentieth-century analysis is an improvement on the thirteenth-century one, if only because it makes it easier to see *why* something that Aquinas thought is true, *is* true.

As I expect you will have noticed, to say that understanding is not an operation of the brain, of the *imaginatio*, a *phantasma*, but nonetheless has to be accompanied by some such physical operations, *phantasmata*, is not unlike saying that the meaning of a word is not a physical property of a word, like its sound or length, but nonetheless the meaning needs some word or other in some language with some sound or length for it to be the meaning of that word. In other words the problem is very much the same whether we see it in terms of the physical, individual, material *brain* and its relation to the concept or in terms of the physical, individual, material *word* and its relation to its meaning. (Remember, once more, that I am using 'word' to mean any conventional sign: a flag or a symbolic road-sign is a word in this sense.) If you say, as I do, that a thought cannot be a physical operation of the brain because a meaning cannot be a physical part of a word, you haven't really explained anything; you have just shifted the same problem to a new area.

It is just that it is only a *theory* firstly that I have a brain (you'd have to do something like cut me open to find out) and another *theory* that it has anything to do with thinking. (Most biblical writers after all attribute what we say the brain does— thinking—to the heart, and what we say the heart does, as seat of emotions, to the bowels.) The advantage of starting from the language end is that it is not a *theory* that I use words to communicate. It is an observable fact. Nor is it a theory that the value of words in communication is established by convention and not a physical property of the words. Words are just more obvious and available than things that go on under my skull.

May we just pause for a moment here and try to remember where we are going and where we are at. I'm still engaged (in case you have, forgivably, not noticed) in trying to explain what Aquinas thought about *prudentia* because for him it has an absolutely central place in discussing human action and, in particular, virtuous human action. *Prudentia* is the acquired (or infused) disposition of the *mind* to do well the job of deciding *what to do about achieving* some good *end* that we *desire*: it is 'right practical reason'. I have said that *prudentia* is a practical wisdom about human actions and, since human actions are always concrete and individual (they are not like rules), practical wisdom cannot be simply an intellectual disposition like mathematics, or for that matter any other science; it must involve also our sense knowledge and sense experience. Of course the physical sciences *arise* from particular concrete experiences, but they are not *about* particular concrete experiences. So it seems important to look at sense knowledge, and here we find in Aquinas an interesting discussion of the interior senses, which he says have to be well disposed (just as our will has to be well disposed) if I am to be practically wise— to have *prudentia* and thus be able to make real decisions which are actually my own, coming from me because of what I am, what I have made of myself, or what God has made of me by grace, or both.

We have first looked at the 'co-ordinating sense', the *sensus communis*, an operation (as we should now say) of the brain because of which what we perceive sensually are not isolated colours, sounds, smells, and so on, but gestalts, organized patterns of sensation such that we sensually perceive *objects* and thus objects *over against* ourselves, such that, quite apart from intellect, we and other animals have a sensual self-awareness. A cat senses that it is distinct from its world. This notion is to be contrasted with Descartes's insistence that I know myself only by being conscious of my *thought* and that other animals are simply machines. Aquinas, in any case, thought that even our *intellectual* awareness of self-identity is not simply a consciousness of our act of consciousness but is a reflection on our understanding of the nature of other material things beyond us. In general Aquinas (and much recent modern thinking) attributes to the sensibility that we share with other animals a great deal of what in post-Renaissance thought had to be the job of the conscious mind.

After considering the *sensus communis*, by which we perceive the sensible structures of the world, Aquinas looks at the way such perceptions are available to us when we are no longer actually sensing these structures, and this is the *imaginatio*. But he also talks about the 'evaluative sense' by which we and many of our fellow-animals are sensually aware of the importance of the objects we sense to our bodily lives. This *sensus aestimativus* is a genetically supplied programme by which, as Aquinas usually puts it, 'the sheep seeing the wolf wants to run away, not because it finds the wolf unpleasant to look at but because it is its natural enemy'. It is easy to see how such instincts would come about by natural selection: sheep lacking them would have very short time, if any, for breeding. It is clear that the cultivation and discipline by human animals of such instinctual feelings will be relevant to the intelligent decision that is the work of *prudentia*. The tendencies evoked by the evaluation of the perceived gestalts in the *sensus aestimativus* are retained and deepened in the last of the interior senses, the *sense-memory*, somewhat as the inputs of the *sensus communis* have been retained in the *imaginatio*. The significance for its bodily life that the animal perceives and retains sensually includes, says Aquinas somewhat enigmatically, a sense of the pastness of the experience. This is, I suppose, a part of the significance of the experience: that it actually happened and that it happened recently or long ago. The *imaginatio* does not, for him, have the same link with autobiography; the *phantasmata* carry no link with their own origins. You can, in this sense, imagine a scene without imagining your own presence to it. You can imagine gold mountains you could not have been present to. To claim to remember a scene is to claim to have been there. Here's the picture:

	Received in	*Retained in*
Sensual account of world	*sensus communis*	*imaginatio*
Sensual evaluation of world (for me)	*sensus aestimativus*	*sense-memory*

Aquinas distinguishes two senses of 'memory': intellectual memory and sense-memory. To have learnt and not forgotten that Paris is in France is to have an intellectual memory. This means that if asked where Paris is you will be able to answer the question. It is in your mind but not something that is always before your mind; it is in your mind as a potentiality. You can call up such a memory more or less at will.

A little more about intellectual memory—*and* sense-memory. Before you learnt French you were *able to do so* while your cat or your overcoat was not able to do so. When you have learnt French you will *be able* to read it in a way that someone who merely *can* learn French but has not done so cannot. There are thus two senses here of 'being able to'. The man who can learn French but has not done so simply has the power to learn French (which the cat has not). The one who has learnt French but is not actually using it has not only the power but also the *skill*. But this skill is still one that can be exercised, but may not actually be exercised at a particular time. 'He has a skill in reading French even while he is asleep' makes perfect sense. (Of course, 'even while he is asleep' is an adverbial phrase modifying the verb 'can', not the verb 'read'. [While he is asleep] he can read French. But it is not true that he can [read French while he is asleep].)

So to have a linguistic skill is to have something in your intellectual memory—though it is not, of course, the only case of intellectual memory. You can have such an intellectual memory of anything that you have known, such as somebody's telephone number. To recall an intellectual memory is an act of the intellect but like all acts of human thinking it is accompanied by an operation of the interior sense and can be impeded by whatever impedes the operation of this sense.

Aquinas does not discuss, so far as I know (anyway, not in his commentary on Aristotle's *On Memory and Recollection*), what it is to remember the words of a song, or, even more mysteriously, a tune. It is certainly often easier to get a song (or a hymn) right if you do *not* think about it than if you do. Learning and remembering a song is perhaps more like acquiring a bodily skill than is either learning physics or remembering a phone number, but clearly all of these involve some kind of imposing a pattern on circuits of brain cells. And perhaps sense-memory and intellectual memory are necessarily entangled and merge into one another. One crucial difference remains, however, at least for Aquinas. For him only sense-memory can deal with *the past as such*. Remembering that 2 plus 2 is 4 is quite different from remembering when you first came to Oxford, because the latter is remembering what it was like *at that time* to have an experience while the former is exercising or being able to exercise an intellectual skill. Perhaps it is this way: you remember first arriving in Oxford and you locate it in the past just because it happened to *you*. Having a sense of pastness, as Aquinas calls it, may be closely related to the fact that sense-memory is concerned with recalling your life-narrative, your autobiography, what it was like to experience something yourself. You can know (intellectually) that the Battle of Hastings happened in 1066; you cannot by sense-memory *remember* it happening in 1066—though you may remember the occasion of being told that it happened in 1066.

Incidentally, one of Anthony Kenny's reasons for thinking that interior senses are not really senses is that we cannot be mistaken about the inputs of our interior senses. I can be mistaken about what I see or hear, but I cannot be mistaken about what I imagine, he says. But, if I cannot be wrong, then I cannot be right either. The inner senses are not, for Kenny, sources of information.[1] But our sense-memory can and *does* deceive us and it is quite possible publicly to verify or falsify it, just as it is with, say, sight.

If I am right in thinking that the sense-memory is peculiarly concerned with how we remember *ourselves*, it would seem to me not at all absurd to suggest that the accuracy of our sensual account of ourselves can be a *moral* question. There are surely virtues and vices, mainly those pertaining to the emotions (the ones that come under temperateness and courage), which govern the ways in which by sense-memory we remember our lives: what we hide from ourselves and what we are prepared to admit. It is not difficult to see how self-indulgence, self-deception, or courageous honesty can make important differences to both deliberation and decision, both of which are the field of operation of *prudentia*, which is concerned, remember, with the *means* we take to an end. In *deliberation*, I have suggested, we are concerned with surveying the possible means to the ends we seek to achieve, and I argued that this is in great part a matter of selecting the relevant information to take into account. You may remember that in discussing means–ends reasoning in Chapter 10 I followed Kenny in noting that it was not, like theoretical reasoning, 'truth-preserving', but rather 'satisfactoriness-preserving', and was concerned not with what it is necessary to do to achieve an

---

[1] Anthony Kenny, *Aquinas on Mind* (London: Routledge, 1993), p. 39.

end, but rather with what is sufficient. I pointed out that whereas the truth of the conclusion of a theoretical syllogism, once it is seen necessarily to follow from the truth of the premisses, is unaffected by adding further premisses or any additional information, the satisfactoriness of the conclusion of a means–ends syllogism is affected by the satisfactoriness of additional premisses ('But how will this affect poor Aunt Jemima?', etc.). So perhaps it is beginning to appear how the way we have stocked and ordered the storehouses of our *imaginatio* and our sense-memory, and the extent to which we are willing honestly to look into them, will be of great importance to the exercise of *prudentia* in our deliberation and equally important to our decision, our choice of what to do, bearing in mind who and what kind of a character we really are.[2]

Aquinas discusses intellectual memory in the Prima Pars of the *Summa Theologiae*, shortly after he has talked about memory as a sense power, and he takes the opportunity to say something about where he stands in relation to the great eleventh-century Persian Islamic philosopher Ibn-Sina (Avicenna to the West). As I have said several times, Aquinas believed that my thoughts could not be mine in the sense that my toenails are mine. Meanings, which are the form of my thoughts, cannot be my personal property, existing hidden inside my head. Meanings are public because they belong to the language, and language must, of its nature, be public. As Kenny suggests, it would not make sense to say that one person was, by a lucky mutation, born with a capacity for language unless there were others with a capacity for language. Meanings exist because of the agreed conventions amongst people that *this* shall be the meaning of *that* symbol. To know the meaning of a word is to know the conventional rules for its use. How such conventions arise remains, as I have said, profoundly mysterious. A tribe could not, for example, have

---

[2] Cf. *Summa Theologiae*, 1a, 79, 6.

called a council to decide these matters—you cannot call a council and discuss such conventions (as you might call one to decide to drive on the left or right side of the road) because you cannot *call* a council and discuss anything until you already have a language and the conventions are already in place.

So my words do not mean whatever I want them to mean or 'intend' them to mean; they mean what, by social convention, they mean in the public language. Of course, once they exist their meanings can be modified by the creativity or laziness of people (creativity enriches a language; laziness, by not bothering to make distinctions and treating as synonyms words which are not, simply impoverishes a language by diminishing its vocabulary).

Now Avicenna, noticing that meanings are not the private property of anybody's mind, decided that they existed only in a common universal Mind. This was, at least, a degree more sophisticated than the empiricist notion that ideas are simply bodily processes like sensations—and something like Avicenna's thought was resurrected in our own time in structuralism, in which the works of, say, Shakespeare are the product of the language and culture of his time operating through him. So, for Avicenna, a thought is mine only indirectly, when the material *phantasma* which always accompanies actual thought is mine and in my head.

Perhaps I should insert a word here about the *intellectus possibilis* (which I like to call the 'receptive mind' and some call the 'recipient intellect') and the *intellectus agens* (which I like to call the 'creative mind' and some call the 'abstractive intellect'). I think it is best and simplest to translate this into modern terms. Our having a *receptive* mind is, as I see it, just our being linguistic animals, our having a capacity for language and hence thought. The *creative* mind is our active capacity to *make* a language, to establish by convention the rules for the use of certain sounds and shapes as symbols with an accepted meaning.

We are presented in our experience with gestalts arising

from the operation of the exterior and interior senses, all of which I call the sensual interpretation of our world. I have frequently stressed that our experience is well-cooked by our bodily senses by the time we receive it: it is there ready to guide us in coping with the world. And when I say 'us' I mean not just ourselves but our fellow-animals. Our experiences, whether actually happening or stored as *phantasmata* in the *imaginatio*, are, in our human case, illuminated by the creative mind. This means, in my terminology, that we create words, create a language, for expressing our sensual experience: we take it up into language.

Those who call the *intellectus agens* (my 'creative mind') the 'abstractive intellect' do so because the medieval and scholastic way of talking about what I have called 'taking experience up into language' is 'abstracting the intelligible species from the phantasm'. I regard this as dangerous talk, not because it is wrong but because since the seventeenth century (or earlier) it has been highly misleading. It has led to 'abstractionism'. The best and most forthright criticism of abstractionism is by Peter Geach in sections 6–11 of his excellent little book *Mental Acts*. He begins:

> I shall use 'abstractionism' as a name for the doctrine that a concept is acquired by a process of singling out in attention some one feature given in direct experience— *abstracting* it—and ignoring the other features simultaneously given—*abstracting from* them ... My own view is that abstractionism is wholly mistaken; that no concept at all is acquired by the supposed process of abstraction.[3]

That is my view too.

---

[3] Peter Geach, *Mental Acts* (London: Routledge and Kegan Paul, 1957), p. 18.

Chapter 14

Moral Virtues I

Time is running out so now I shall confine myself to talking about what Aquinas calls the 'moral virtues', meaning the dispositions of our appetitive powers, our powers of being attracted, which he distinguishes from intellectual virtues such as *prudentia*, practical wisdom, which is a disposition of our powers of understanding—though one with immediate practical moral implications. A preliminary thing I would like to do is clear up unfinished business regarding what Aquinas has to say about the two kinds of memory we have: sense-memory, which is one of the interior senses, and intellectual memory, which is simply what we have in mind, what we have learnt and not forgotten. Then I would like to talk about the moral virtue that governs our *intellectual* appetite, the will (*voluntas*), the appetite which is attracted by the world as understood, as linguistically interpreted, as talked about; and, later, the virtues which have to do with our sensual appetites, the desires and emotions evoked by the world as sensually interpreted. These latter virtues are divided by Aristotle and Aquinas into two groups: those that deal with our appetites of simple desire, desire for food and drink and sex (coping, you might say, with the pleasures of life)—temperateness—and those that deal with our appetites of aggression (coping with the difficulties of life)—courage and patience.

First, though, as a hangover from the last chapter, a further word about intellectual memory. This is memory that originates in the past *understanding* of sense experience, the linguistic account we give of it, whereas sense-memory is recalling the sense experience itself. The sense-memory has thus an essential content of pastness. By contrast, in order to have in your *intellectual* memory the fact that Germany is larger than Switzerland you do not have to remember the occasion in the past when you first discovered this truth. I have been suggesting that sense-memory is fundamentally a capacity to know your own life-story (to know sensually—for this is a power we share with non-linguistic animals). What Aquinas calls a sense of 'pastness' is being able to locate, to some degree, a section of your life-story in its proper order. The essential point that Aquinas is making against one who had a great influence on his early thought (i.e. Avicenna) is that we *can* have thoughts that we are not attending to. For Avicenna, because thought has no physical organ (and here, of course, Aquinas agrees with him), no material component which can retain an imprint, thoughts can only exist when they are actually being thought. For Aquinas, however, the difference between someone who has learnt some truth but is not actually considering it, and somebody who has not yet learnt it, is most simply accounted for by speaking of two stages of actualization. There is that actualization of the intellect which amounts to having acquired a skill, and a further actualization that is the use of this skill. And it is to make this point that he talks of intellectual memory. For Aquinas, to learn a truth is for the creative mind to actualize the receptive mind with a particular linguistic interpretation of the world, and this then exists in the receptive mind as a disposition or intellectual skill. For Aquinas it was important that the receptive mind (the capacity for language) and the creative mind (the actual deployment of the symbols of a particular language in which the world is to be interpreted) are faculties of each human individual. He distanced himself from his more Neoplatonic masters St Augustine (with his notion of 'illumination') and Avicenna, for whom the creative mind was something

144

transcending individuals (and for Augustine, was divine). In this Aquinas was much more like modern Aristotelians such as Gilbert Ryle or Peter Geach.

For the exercise of practical wisdom in deciding what to do we need, then, on this view, both intellectual memory (because it is a matter of reason) and sense-memory (because it is *practical* reason and thus concerned with our experience of and sensitivity to individual events). In *prudentia* we bring our experience as well as our understanding to bear upon our present concrete individual situation. But there I have to leave *prudentia* for the moment. It is that particular use of *reason* which, you might say, Aquinas believes in instead of the so-called 'voice of conscience' of later writers.

Let us now have a rather quick look at the right disposition of the will, the intellectual appetite, the virtue or rather the cluster of virtues that we call justice.

Aquinas begins his discussion of justice with the notion of the *ius*, a kind of equality, or equalizing between people. The *ius* is what is due to a person, and here we find what, for Aquinas, is the proper place of obligation in ethics. Unlike moral philosophers in the tradition of Kant, Aristotle notoriously says hardly anything about obligation and law in the *Nicomachean Ethics*; if you had duties or obligations they sprang from some status or niche in society, but they were certainly not the foundation of ethics. Aquinas writes in a similar spirit: Daniel Westberg has remarked on the great distance Aquinas puts (simply in terms of numbers of pages) between his treatment of human action (and what makes an action good or bad) and his treatment of law.[1] Of course, much more important to Aquinas than the influence of Aristotle is the tradition of the Bible and here there is a strong emphasis on the Torah, the law, which seems identified with righteousness. Aquinas is absolutely clear that the moral prescriptions of the

---

[1] Daniel Westberg, *Right Practical Reason: Aristotle, Action, and Prudence in Aquinas* (Oxford: Clarendon Press, 1994).

Old Law (as distinct from the ceremonial or ritual prescriptions, which belong to the era of types and shadows, sacrifices which have been made out of date by the cross of Christ) hold, that the moral prescriptions of the Decalogue retain all their force for Christians. This is because, for Aquinas, the Ten Commandments have to do with safeguarding the life of virtues and friendship. But for him, 'That which is most important in the law of the New Testament and that in which its whole power consists is the grace of the Holy Spirit that is given through faith in Christ'.[2] The Decalogue is in large part a written expression of the boundaries of human friendship. The New Law is the presence in us of divine friendship, the Holy Spirit.

With the notion of justice comes that of rights. Indeed 'right' is often used as a translation of *ius*. Justice is thus directed against whatever makes for domination, bullying, treating others as without rights.

Justice, for Aquinas, is the stable disposition to give everyone his or her due; it is concerned with maintaining an equality between people. Thus if you lend me twenty pounds there is created a kind of inequality. So long as you have *your* money and I have *mine* there is an equality there (even if you have a lot more than I have). Aquinas calls this a proportional equality. If *I* have twenty pounds of *your* money there is a certain inequality which is dissolved by my paying you the money back.

Because of this basis in equality Aquinas held that justice in the strict sense cannot apply between natural unequals. So, for example, he thought it would be stretching language to speak of children's rights against their parents. There can only be justice here 'imperfectly'. Children, he thought, were not sufficiently distinct, sufficiently 'other' from their parents to stand in a relation of equality with them. There is a natural relationship between parents and children, a *philia* that is

---

[2] *Summa Theologiae*, 1a2ae, 106, 1.

much more profound and important than justice, which does not depend on any contract in the way that, say, a loan does.

As we shall see, he would think it a mere metaphor to speak of 'animal rights'. Our treatment of animals and communication with them needs to be governed by more complex considerations than legal justice. Talk of 'animal rights' comes from a culture which cannot see morality in terms other than rights, duties, and obligations.

Among the most interesting cases of inequality which precludes strict justice is that of God and his human creatures. For Aquinas, the virtue of 'religion' is a special case of imperfect justice. But more of this later.

Justice, then, is essentially about a relation to another and its criteria are objective, unlike the virtues that concern the sensual appetites. These latter concern your emotions and feelings. 'It ain't what you do, it's the way that you do it,' as the old song says. Two people may both eat and drink in moderate amounts, but one might do it because he lives in an institution that provides that kind of meal, and with the other it might be that he simply does not want to be greedy and infantile about such matters: he has the virtue of temperateness. Most virtues take quite a long time to acquire and in the earlier stages we may have mainly external motives for behaving well; we do not have the virtue until it has become 'second nature' so to do.

Now it is important to see that such considerations apply quite differently to justice. It is true that we will not be truly just until acting justly becomes second nature to us, part of our 'character', so that we do not pay our debts or whatever reluctantly and with bad grace. But justice is not *about* the way in which we act but what it is that we do.

A man might while mildly drunk do some act which it would ordinarily take a brave man to do, but it would not be an act of courage; it would simply resemble one. The man has conquered his fear not by the virtue of courage but by inebriation (Dutch courage). On the other hand, someone who has to be mildly drunk before he can bring himself to pay his debts *is* acting justly.

Whether a person is chaste or a glutton is a psychological question. Whether he is just or not is a social question. So justice is concerned with social relationships.

Aquinas first distinguishes what he calls *particular justice*, which is justice towards an individual, but I think he would be fully prepared to speak of particular justice towards an institution or an ethnic group or whatever. He makes this distinction really for the sake of saying a word about what he calls *general justice*, by which he means any human behaviour seen in terms of its social implications. 'General justice', he says, 'commands all the other virtues', which is simply to say that all human behaviour has a political resonance. He does not mean that temperateness or steadfastness are a kind of justice but that they belong to the common good and so their cultivation makes a contribution to the common good, so that justice to the whole community demands them.

You may remember that Aristotle, in distinguishing what makes the relationship of fellow-citizens different from trade relations and military agreements with foreigners, says that fellow-citizens are united by *philia*: a friendship based on sharing a life of a common pursuit of virtue. That means that in a healthy political society people will be concerned for the flourishing of their fellow-citizens which comes from virtue— concerned, that is, for health and education as a matter for the whole community. It is because we have lost the significance and strength of the word 'virtue' that being concerned for a fellow-citizen's virtue sounds priggish; if we said 'concern for their human happiness' it would sound better.

General justice, then, Aquinas says, directs all our virtues towards the good of *social* life, just as he will later say that charity directs all our virtues to the good of *divine* life. But now let us look at individual particular justice. This is itself distinguished not according to the object it is directed to but according to the agent who practises it. Justice between one

individual and another individual is *commutative justice*; the
justice owed by *society* to an individual is *distributive justice*.
(Remember that in both these cases, for 'individual' we can
also read 'institution' or 'group'.)

The notion of distributive justice is the one unfamiliar in our
world except as an accusation: 'You think that society owes
you a living.' This is precisely what Aristotle thought. The
whole community, in a real society, will be concerned about
the welfare and flourishing of all its members simply because
they are members. For Aristotle, a just society, practising
distributive justice, has a stake in every member, and every
member has a stake in the society. This differs sharply from the
views of those who speak contemptuously of the 'nanny state'
(these belong, for the most part, to the small but influential
group of people who can afford to remember what nannies
were). These believe that, so far as possible, services to the
community as a whole should be based on commutative rather
than distributive justice. That is the theory of the almost
universal superiority of privatization to public provision. It
seems to me, if I may declare an interest, that it is perfectly
plausible that the exercise of *distributive* justice itself might quite
often suggest encouraging and controlling private enterprise
operating in terms of commutative transactions in particular
fields, the whole thing depending on the prudential judgement
of the authorities, of course taking a whole lot of factors into
account and not just windfalls from the sale of assets or large
salaries for managers, as one does in any prudential judgement. The making of such practical judgements rather than
the imposition of pre-formed theoretical views or doctrines
seems to me what authorities are for. And with this Aquinas
certainly agrees.

Commutative justice, or what we might translate as 'fair
trading', is not left by Aquinas simply to the operations of the
market. It is not only individual moral behaviour but also
business transactions that are subject to unpredictable
circumstances—catastrophic droughts and floods and all kinds

of accidents and chances which may lead to desperate hardship for many who are too poor to have leverage in the market. Aquinas is clear that in such cases distributive justice requires of the state that it intervene to fix both prices and wages. But for him distributive justice is not involved in just *any* action by society as a whole, or the state, upon individuals. Indeed, the origin of the concept lies in the distribution of honours to worthy citizens. It seems clear that the notion of meriting an honour is central to this, and it is not an easy concept for us to grasp. Aquinas says that while commutative justice is solely concerned with the value of *things*, distributive justice has to take into account the value of *persons*.[3]

Now he cannot possibly mean by this the value of individuals without any context. There is a fundamental sense in which the value of an individual 'for whom Christ died', as Paul put it, is simply incommensurable with the value of anything else; what Aquinas has to be talking about is a certain kind of *social* value. Perhaps we can approach this idea if we think about how disgusting it is to speak of the value of a slave in a slave market, and yet how appropriate it is to speak of the value of Mozart or Einstein or Mother Theresa. To say it again, there is always in the background the mystery of sanctity—which is a matter of God's love for individuals (for, of course, in Aquinas's view God does not love people more for being saints, they are saints because he loves them more; but this is not something that we can judge or ought to pretend to judge). What we are talking about here is something between the mere utility by which we would assess the value of a slave, and the sanctity which we cannot assess at all. Even in the most democratic and egalitarian society there is a sense (not, to repeat, an absolute, *sub specie aeternitatis* sense) in which some people are more important than others to the community. The very fact that we may deplore the importance given temporarily to, say, pop stars suggests that there are some

---

[3] *Summa Theologiae*, 2a2ae, 61, 1–3.

other people we think more important; so the notion makes some kind of sense to us.

So long as we do not absolutize this into an idolatry or trivialize it into snobbery, this does seem to be an enduring (though hard to analyse) feature of social life. Anyway it seems clear that some such evaluation of our fellow-citizens is at the primitive roots of the notion of distributive justice. It is not just about providing social services to all; it has to do with rewarding those who have deserved well of the community. And the honour we pay them is not just esteem but more material. Nobel and Booker Prize winners get richer as well as more famous. Be that as it may, let us now go back to what the community as a whole owes to *all* its members. Aquinas advances two contrasting propositions. The first is that the human individual is essentially a *part* of society and hence the common good of society is greater than the good of the individual. The second is that society exists for the sake of the good life of its citizens. This second proposition entails, I shall argue, that there are certain kinds of behaviour towards its citizens that a society cannot authorize without thereby ceasing to be a true society: that is, one without authority at least in this case.

Let us suppose that a doctor is confronted by a patient suffering from persistent mysterious headaches. If none of the usual remedies seems to work, the doctor will search the literature and seek advice from consultant specialists and so on. Now it is quite clear that one thoroughly effective way of ensuring that the patient does not have any more of these headaches is to cut his head off. This, however, the doctor will not prescribe: not because it is less effective than other remedies but because it is outside his competence as a doctor. He might do it, of course, but not *qua* doctor. It is outside his competence because of what it *means* to be a doctor, which entails the limited task of seeking to restore health. It is quite possible that the patient, tormented by his headaches, might decide to end them by suicide, but in doing so he would not be *doctoring* himself. It is not within the scope of what it means to be a doctor, as such, to kill the patient; there would be a contradiction or absurdity in describing this as medical treatment. So, in one way, it would be absurd to seek to cure the headache by repeating the Lord's Prayer backwards at the time of the full moon, because it wouldn't work: it is not the kind of means that would achieve that end. It would also be equally absurd, in another way, to try to cure it by decapitation, because this is not the kind of thing that curing is. Now just as it means something quite specific to be a doctor, so it means something quite specific to be a *polis*, a human society, and quite parallel considerations apply to both. There are limits to what can be done by a doctor as such and limits on what can be done by a human society as such.

Just as it would be a contradiction for a doctor to prescribe decapitation, so it would be a contradiction for the state, the authority in society, to want to *harm* its citizens. When this happens (as it does) the state is to this extent bogus. The people with power are simply pretending to be what the authority of the society is. *Tolerating* harm is not the same as wanting to inflict it. We may often have to tolerate harm in order to prevent a greater harm. Aquinas asks whether the laws of a state ought to command every good action (in the sense of approving of it) and he says 'Yes'; civil law is about morality in that sense. He then asks whether civil law should forbid every bad action and he says 'No'. Civil law is distinct from morality in this sense. Civil law is for the sake of the common good. It is quite often the case, he points out, that making a morally bad action illegal will do more harm to the common good than tolerating it. We might note in passing the difference between the modern use of 'toleration' and the medieval one. In modern English tolerance is a virtue and means not persecuting people simply because they are different from you, because they may be good. In medieval terms it means not prosecuting people who are doing things you are quite sure are evil. Toleration is not here a virtue but simply a concession to the necessary limitations of human law. Thus, for example, there is nothing logically odd about tolerating legal abortion and thinking it a great evil.

So a society, just because of what it is, cannot as such approve the harming of citizens. What it can do, however, is seek to prevent its citizens from harming each other or harming society as a whole. Primarily this is done by ensuring that people are educated in the virtues and acquire that maturity that is an essential part of the good life. But secondly, because such education is liable to fail in individual cases, so that people grow up either immature or with developed vices such as avarice and ambition, the state has to use the threat of punishment to preserve its citizens from harm. Punishment, just as much as education or a health system, has to do with preventing harm to the citizens of the society. This is its *meaning*, and, as such, its meaning is in no contradiction to the meaning of society itself. Now the act of punishment may, and quite often will, involve harm to the criminal, who is a citizen, but this is incidental to it. Essentially it is not a matter of harming but preventing harm to citizens. Harming the criminal is no part of the meaning of punishment, as pain is no part of the meaning of childbirth and exhaustion is no part of the meaning of winning the London Marathon. What is essential to punishment is not harm but coercion: that you should be doing to the criminal something that he or she does not want done. And this is simply so that most people will refrain from criminality on the grounds that they do not want this to happen to them. There is nothing logically odd about doing things to people which they do not want done but which, in fact, do them no harm. Our minds are confused about this. We confuse harm and coercion (punishment) and this is no doubt because during the last three centuries our preferred form of punishment has been imprisonment, which is both disliked and also normally does immeasurable harm to people. Conversely, of course, it is quite possible to do people harm while doing something they do not fear at all, but rather welcome. To make crack or heroin freely available to an addict would harm and possibly kill him, and it would not serve as a punishment because he would presumably welcome it. So punishment (even capital punishment in the almost inconceivable circumstances in which it might function for preventing crime) does not have the *meaning* of harming citizens.

So, although the state that is true to itself cannot directly seek to harm its citizens, in the case of serious criminals who represent a deliberate threat to the order and peace of society, it can rationally propose to coerce them and do things to them which they dislike a lot, and this may, as a matter of incidental fact, involve harming them.

It was to make this distinction between those whom the state may rationally coerce in this way, even though it produces incidental harm, and those to whom it would be irrational (inconsistent with being what the state is) to do so, that the concept of the *in-nocens* was created.

The *in-nocens* (the non-harming) is the non-criminal ordinary citizen. Such innocence does not directly have to do with being a saint (or non-sinner) though, of course, in a just society and even in a society in some respects unjust, being a criminal, breaking the law, does involve being *pro tem* a sinner. Being innocent refers to *not breaking the law* and thus not being liable to coercive punishment in a just society. Later the notion will be extended. One way of putting this is that the *in-nocens* has the *ius* or right not to be harmed or punished by the state. This is, of course, a minimalist statement, for the *in-nocens* has a right, as a matter of distributive justice, to all the benefits produced by living in society. The society exists precisely to provide her or him with these advantages. We called the former South Africa and Nazi Germany unjust because in practice (and sometimes even in theory) they denied this truth.

Rights, in the sense in which Aquinas speaks of them, have meaning only in the context of social life. This is not to say, as positivist lawyers would, that the meaning of rights is simply what happens to be legislated for in a particular society. Aquinas, as we have seen, regards certain rights as a matter of what is reasonable, society being what it is, and allows that it is sometimes reasonable to tolerate and legalize unreasonable activity. Positivists are people who think there is no such thing in nature as what something essentially is; it is simply a matter of what a particular culture takes something to be.

For Aquinas, as I was saying, children only have rights in what he calls an *imperfect* sense because they are not *yet* citizens of the society. Animals can only be said to have rights in a *metaphorical* sense in that they are not members of society at all. They are nevertheless part of our social world and treating them with kindness and compassion has what I earlier called political resonance and thus is part of *general* justice, though kindness and compassion are in themselves exercises in the virtue of temperateness rather than justice. I think that the 'animal rights' people spoil a good case against the abominable things we do to our non-linguistic fellow-animals in laboratories, farms, and factories by trying to force all moral goodness and badness into the legalistic straitjacket of rights in justice. For Aristotle and Aquinas human society itself is based on something deeper than justice, the human solidarity we call *philia*, which is the necessary context of justice. To get a true perspective on our fellow-animals, what we need is not an analogue of social justice but of social *philia*. There can and should be a companionship and solidarity with other animals, which is more an analogue of friendship than citizenship.

Aquinas thought that the rights established by positive law are founded in reason, which he saw as a kind of participation in the wisdom of God. Our *prudentia* is a kind of sharing in divine *providentia*, which he also called 'natural law'. This Aquinas conceives of as distinct from local positive laws devised for particular cultures, and thus he recognized what nowadays are called 'human rights'. For him this was a coherent, intellectually respectable view because it presupposed that the entire human race formed a quasi-political community under the sovereignty of God, who as the author of nature and humanity is the authority for natural and human rights. It is not at all clear that 'human rights' as currently understood can make any sense if deprived of this metaphysical foundation. It would seem that the only way an atheist could make sense of human rights is to see them as a development of positive international law, established by agreement between nations. Of course a Christian sees such human rights as not simply based on the comprehensive authority of the Creator but on the authority of Christ and foreshadowing in a non-sacramental way the coming of the Kingdom, as the Church does in a sacramental way.

Chapter 15

Moral Virtues II

The virtues we shall be looking at very summarily, and in conclusion, are dispositions of sensual appetites and emotions. These dispositions incline us to desire and to feel reasonably. As I have said before, this does not mean that they incline us to reason about our emotions, though we may do so sometimes, but that we have learnt to integrate our desires and passions into the *whole* of our life-experience (instead of letting them take off on a life of their own), so that we are inclined to do, we feel like doing, what is reasonable and leads to happiness. These are dispositions of our emotions themselves. They are not a matter of some overarching power called the will by which we may dominate our emotions. Aquinas says reason should be in charge, but like a constitutional monarch, not a tyrant. When we have to make a great effort to control our emotions it is a sign that we lack the virtues in question. And we all begin lacking them. There *are* dispositions of our desires that spring not from what we are sensually aware of but just from our *intellectual* assessment of the world; these are the cool virtues associated with justice. There are, thought Aquinas, a reasonable and an unreasonable time, place, and way of being afraid or angry or sexually attracted or militant; and if by good upbringing, and quite difficult training, our emotional life is disposed to what is in fact reasonable then we shall discover the happiness of mature human life.

Aquinas believed that in this matter we start with the cards somewhat stacked against us; we do not begin from, so to say, a position of neutrality. The education of the emotions has first to cope not merely with a *lack* of virtues (as the science teacher starts with pupils who lack physics) but with a certain inherited, or at least somehow 'given', disorder in our emotional life; we start life with an emotional *handicap* which is not necessarily crippling but which needs to be taken account of. What this entails is that without a deliberate, reasonable educational programme we will remain emotionally infantile, unco-ordinated, maladjusted and inclined to irrational action; we will fail to discover mature human love and life. And, as we shall see, Aquinas thought that we needed much more than an educational programme. Unlike Aristotle, he believed not only in human weakness and defect but 'sin' and he spoke of divine grace. Be that as it may, though, for him, as for Aristotle, behaving naturally (in accordance with human nature) did not mean simply 'doing what comes naturally' (i.e. easily). In this, Aristotle and Aquinas belong to the camp of Marx and Freud rather than to that of those more optimistic liberals who thought that if left to herself and uncorrupted by artificial conventions and institutions, a person would just naturally be good, humane, and reasonable.

I think it is important to notice here that everybody who engages with this matter seems to agree that there is something gravely the matter with the human animal simply in comparison with other animals. If you ask the question: what is the most dangerous wild animal?, the answer is, as everyone agrees, the human one. If you look at, say, the destruction of the ozone layer, or the greenhouse effect, at acid rain and the wholesale destruction of rainforests, and all the other lamentably fashionable disasters, it really does begin to look as though the arrival of the linguistic animal on the evolutionary scene was simply a grave calamity for the earth. Human beings seem simply not to be properly fitted for life on earth. In the past, before we got a real stranglehold on the planet, people could fail to see this, and were able to imagine that once we had got a few things right, and especially when science had developed a bit more, and pushed back the frontiers of ignorance, human beings would be able to live easily enough in harmony with nature. Now, however, when technology *has* developed in the hoped-for way, it is almost impossible not to recognize that the human race is engaged in destroying the planet it is sitting on.

The thing gets even more peculiar when we realize that the human race seems not simply hostile to the earth, and bent on destroying it. This species seems also deeply devoted to destroying itself. No other animal species known to me carries on murder and war and self-destruction in the way that we do. Of course most of *all* animal living is about killing and being killed, even if you are only thinking of killing plants. What is much rarer is intra-specific killing, killing members of your own species, race-suicide. It happens, of course, in some species (some rats, for instance), but in most cases such behaviour is due to unusual conditions of overcrowding or other stress. The linguistic animal sometimes behaves as though it lived in a *permanent* condition of stress; and maybe it does. In any case, the sheer scale of the killing makes the human animal a unique case. An enormous proportion of national income, which means an enormous proportion of human working time and energy, is devoted to devising and producing instruments for hurting and killing other human beings.

As I say, so far as I know, nobody nowadays who has looked at the way things are disagrees about all this. They differ only in what they think we ought to and can do about it—which, of course, involves a difference in what they think is the reason for this bizarre phenomenon. First (just to get them out of the way) there are those who simply accept that all this is inevitable (and some of them, notably the Nazis, actually glory in it being so). These are people who think that all life is about perpetual struggle for dominance and that the proper reaction in this situation is to make sure that you and your lot are victorious in the struggle. Quite often these people think that this picture of life as a continual clawing your way to the top has something to do with evolution and even, quite falsely, attribute such notions to Charles Darwin. They even used to call themselves Social Darwinists. I think (though, of course, perhaps wrongly) that this is not so much a line of *thought* as a piece of romantic posturing, like all glorification of violence.

Turning to people who have thought about the matter, Marx and Freud each have their accounts of how we got or get into this peculiar state of affairs. For Marx it has to do with how social and economic life is structured: when a man's work is alienated from him, as in slavery, feudalism, or capitalism, the result is distortion in the way we live together (that is to say, in the way we live). Such distortions are manifested at many levels: political, religious, literary, psychological. For him the solution, therefore, lies in the subversion of dehumanizing, alienating structures by revolution, and he claims to have found a certain rough pattern of such revolutions in the historical transition from slavery, through serfdom, via the enormously bloody and prolonged capitalist revolution, to proletarianism. The next (probably violent) revolution should take us to socialism, which then (though this is quite speculative) by non-violent revolution may ultimately result in communism. Then, the distortions of alienation being removed, human beings will at last be in charge of their own lives. We will have what Marx calls 'the total redemption of humanity'. So Marx's solution, then, is, having understood the way history seems to go, to nudge it along as skilfully as possible. He was not, of course, a mechanistic determinist about history. He thought we would have to work at nudging it.

For Freud, the cause of our maladjustment lies with the family and the traumas of early childhood, and his solution lies in being confronted with, confronting ourselves with, the reality of these events. Both Marx and Freud think we begin with a false picture (and they try to show why this happens).

They also think that we cope unsatisfactorily with our difficulties by systematically deceiving ourselves about them, and living amongst illusions (one of which, of course, is religion). And they believe that any serious cure for the human condition will involve the disappearance of such illusions. For Marx, the 'total redemption of humanity will mean the disappearance of religion'. For him, unlike many nineteenth-century bourgeois atheists, religion was primarily a symptom rather than a cause of the alienated human condition and he didn't think it very important to waste time on attacking it; he expected it simply to wither away even in the socialist phase of history. When you have found the real cure to the disease you no longer need painkillers.

Aquinas, while I think he would have had no difficulty in accommodating both what Marx says about socio-economic structures and perhaps large parts of Freud's perception of childhood, reckons that the roots of human alienation must lie deeper. He traces them, like any traditional Christian, to the very beginning of the human race. He sees the human alienation both from the environment and from fellow-humans as having its source in an alienation from God—essentially in a human rejection of divine love. He sees the maladjustments of human animals, the stunting of their emotional and imagina-tive life (which entails a difficulty in thinking straight), as not itself a sin but what he calls the *material* side of a basic sinfulness or lack of grace, which is *formally* (what its *meaning* is) an absence of friendship with God. If we were simply one animal species amongst others, we might have originated simply as human beings (in the way that giraffes originate simply as giraffes), in which case there would have been no problem of original sin. Life would have had its difficulties and challenges but our emotional life, the sphere of both desire and of aggression, would not have been disordered and somewhat out of touch with the real world as understood by our reason ('linguistically interpreted', in my terminology). But in the utterly mysterious plan of God's love, we were offered a sharing not just in human but in divine life, the life of grace, and (in the even more mysterious plan of God) he permitted us to reject this gift. The consequent disorder of human animals takes on the character of sin because it originated in this rejection and it is a rejection we would in some way be doomed to re-enact in our individual lives by sins we actually commit were it not for the other part of God's plan, which is the renewal of the life of grace through the sanctity of one of us, the man Jesus Christ, who is the historical presence to us of the Word of the eternal God himself.

It is important to recognize that no Christian is subject to original sin. They have all, I think, had their faith (by which they are 'in Christ') sacramentally expressed in baptism or else, being capable of decision, they have expressed it in other ways known only to God. What they are unfortunately subject to is the emotional disorder—what Aquinas calls the *fomes peccati* (the 'tinder' of sin)—which is not sinful but which makes it a more arduous task to acquire virtues than you might expect.

Original sin, by the way, is not so called because of the myth of the origin of humankind in Adam and Eve but because it is a condition we suffer from in our own origin as distinct from the sins we actually commit. In a most interesting article by Michael Nolan, which I strongly recommend to you,[1] there is a useful discussion of Aquinas's view of original sin. Nolan stresses the difference between a Catholic and a Protestant perspective on the matter, particularly the contrast between Aquinas and Luther. I think, myself, that Nolan accepts too readily Luther's interpretation of what Nolan calls the 'scholastic' view of the 'two-tier' character of grace and nature ('the wreath on the head' etc.). Luther, so far as I know, did not read Aquinas. Moreover I think Nolan does not bring out the fact that Aquinas was not, of course, dissociating himself

[1] Michael Nolan, 'Aquinas and the Act of Love', *New Blackfriars*, Vol. 77, No. 902, March 1996, pp. 115–30.

from Protestants but from his enormously influential Catholic master, St Augustine. Nolan gives a good account of 'Limbo', which was invented by Aquinas and his contemporaries precisely to replace Augustine's teaching that unbaptized infants are simply damned. Nor does he note that Augustine associated the 'hereditary' transmission of original sin with being conceived in the disorder of sexual passion. Aquinas will have none of this. He says that it is all the other way round. If we did not suffer from the effects of original sin, we would still have sex but it would be much more passionate and pleasurable.[2]

Aquinas, then, did not think (as Luther did) that it was in human nature to be disordered, but that the confused condition of human beings could be traced to the offer of grace, divine life, being *rejected*. And it is this disorder, for him, that is at the root of those social and personal distortions that, in our own age, have been identified by Marx and Freud. For Aquinas we are not perpetually sinners, but we do suffer throughout this life from the psychological, bodily, and emotional effects of being deprived of a grace which is not, indeed, natural to us, but for which we were intended and are now once more intended in God's plan.

It is a nuisance, you might say, to be born having to carry around with us the corpse of our defeated enemy.

I should say in passing that Aquinas associated the sacramental life and the whole business of organized, institutional religion and, of course, faith with this maladjusted state of our desires and inclinations. For him we have this kind of religion depending wholly upon faith and expressed in special sacred signs because we live in a world that has been distorted by sin and alienation. For this reason he would agree with Karl Marx that religion is indeed a *sign* of human alienation, and that when we come to 'the total redemption of humanity', religion, at least in this sense, will disappear. Faith will be

---

[2] *Summa Theologiae*, 1a, 98, 2.

replaced by vision, and the sacred rites by the secular, perfected by the Spirit. Thus, for Marx, the remedy for the strange human condition lies in the revolutionary restructuring of social and economic life; for Freud in confronting and accepting the truth about ourselves, and especially about our infancy and childhood; but for Aquinas this is not radical enough—the ultimate answer is to be found in the restoration and perfection of our human nature through resurrection, through being given that share in *divine* nature for which we were originally destined.

This restoration has only begun in the period between Christ's resurrection and the parousia. Until then we live by faith and work at the difficult task of growing in virtue and maturity while coping with our emotional and intellectual incompetences. But in all this, by grace we share in the 'infused virtues'—part of our living by the Spirit.

Aristotle was well aware of the difficulties in leading a truly human kind of life, especially before but also even after acquiring the virtues, but of course he does not give this the theological interpretation that Aquinas gets from Scripture. So Aquinas finds him a suitable starting point, but only a starting point, for his development of an account of the virtues of the emotions. As we shall see, he modifies Aristotle's account and develops it at length and with considerable subtlety.

So let us now look at the virtues we need in order to restore and cultivate our emotional life so that we can live as reasonable and satisfied and, in Aquinas's view, ultimately divinized human beings.

Besides, then, the virtue of justice, by which we are disposed to arrange our *life in common*, our social life, in accordance with reason, we need those virtues that dispose us to deal with the *difficulties* we find in behaving reasonably and enjoying life: the difficulties that spring on the one hand from the *dangers* and on the other hand from the *pleasures* of sensual life. At first we are all too inclined both to shun dangers and to seek pleasures even at the expense of reasonable and just action. So we need the virtue of *fortitudo* (courage) disposing our aggressive appetites in the face of what is difficult and dangerous, and the virtue of *temperantia* (temperateness) to dispose our appetites of desire in the face of what is sensually attractive.

FORTITUDO (COURAGE)

It belongs to the virtue of courage, says Aquinas, to 'protect human appetite lest it draw back from what is reasonable through bodily fear.'[3] It must be stressed that for Aquinas the emotions are good things in themselves; both fear and militancy (*timor* and *adduce*) are good and necessary responses to a threat. An animal, human or not, which did not have a healthy respect for dangerous predators, or which lacked all capacity to stand up to them, would be in a defective state and fairly soon dead. The virtue of courage is the disposition to have the right degree of fear and of militancy; it excludes the opposite excesses of timidity and over-aggressiveness. Aquinas agrees with Aristotle that virtue normally aims at a 'mean' between opposite vices.

In practice, as it turns out, the distortion from which we start in our emotional life inclines us more often to fail on the side of cowardice than of rashness; so we tend to think of courage as mainly a matter of being more brave. But we should not forget that it is the same virtue that prevents us from foolishly throwing our lives away in bravado. Aristotle deals with courage mainly as the virtue of the soldier and it is important to remember that soldiering for him was not simply a technique (something for 'professionals'). You were only a soldier in the strict sense if you were fighting for the defence of the *polis*, the community without which there could be no justice, no life of virtue. The good of the whole *polis*, as Aquinas never tires of saying, is greater than any individual's good; hence he agrees with Aristotle that, if we are to define courage

---

[3] *Summa Theologiae*, 2a2ae, 123, 4.

by its greatest exercise, it is risking the greatest personal evil, death, for the sake of the greatest good, the existence and security of the just society.

But, having paid his respects to Aristotle, Aquinas immediately extends the notion of war to the defence of justice *within* the *polis* and speaks of the magistrate or other citizen who is not deterred from administering justice by intimidation by death squads or their equivalent. His paradigm cases would be the Italian magistrates murdered by the Mafia. Aquinas is at some pains to eliminate the 'machismo' element of courage, and for him *sustinere* (endurance without excessive fear) is a greater, because more difficult, exercise of the virtue than is rational militancy or daring. For him, too, patience is an important virtue amongst those that cluster around courage. (It was not a virtue recognized by Aristotle.) For Aquinas the courageous person is essentially steadfast and determined in the midst of difficulties, dangers, and threats, and he devotes a special article to arguing that one does not take *delight* in the exercise of courage.[4] Even more than Aristotle, Aquinas is clearly moving beyond the Homeric warrior ideal. This is of course due to the influence of the New Testament, but it is also worth noticing that Aquinas lived during the transition from the 'heroic', aristocratic, feudal world of the Germanic tribes to the new urban civilization. One of the interests in reading him is to watch him developing a balanced synthesis of ideas and attitudes from both cultures.

In fact Aquinas devotes less space to considering physical courage and the ability to face death than he does to the virtues which he associates with courage because they have to do with what is difficult in the sense of being large-scale and important. He devotes, for example, nineteen articles to a virtue we hardly hear of in our society, that of *magnanimitas*, greatness of soul: a disposition to do the kind of things that win someone public praise. It is not that these things are done for

---

[4] *Summa Theologiae*, 2a2ae, 123, 8.

the *sake* of public praise—ambition and vainglory are discussed by Aquinas as *vices* opposed to *magnanimitas*—but it is the virtue that belongs to good statesmen and politicians (for Aquinas believed there could be such), to people like the engineer Isambard Kingdom Brunel and to James Murray, who compiled the *Oxford English Dictionary*, to Lenin and Bob Geldof, who were ready to face and deal with enormously complex and difficult problems to do something of great public worth.

Although Aquinas thinks that magnanimity can best be understood by considering those who undertake great public achievements, nevertheless he allows that in a sense it can be available to the rest of us in proportion to our opportunities. Although good fortune, wealth, and power contribute to the full expression of magnanimity, essentially it consists in wanting to extend yourself, to operate at full stretch. Amongst the vices opposed to it are *presumptio*, which is biting off more than you can chew, and pusillanimity (small-souledness), which is always biting off less.

Magnanimitas, 'doing things big', is related to a virtue even more unfamiliar to the bourgeois world: *magnificentia*. I think there is a puritan tradition which would find it simply shocking that a Christian preacher should treat *magnificentia* as a virtue. It is an 'aristocratic', even a primitive, virtue, and it means a kind of careless largeness in dealing with possessions which does not calculate how they might be invested but splashes them in great gestures. It is exercised by patrons of the arts and of sports and people who throw great parties, not from mean-minded motives like advertising or vanity but simply from the desire to do something great and difficult (in a smaller way I suppose it is exercised by people who conquer Everest, but *magnificentia* is more directly concerned with using money). Aquinas attaches it to courage not because it has the same subject matter (for courage deals in our fears and our personal safety) but because it exhibits the same kind of attitude to possessions that courage has to life itself.

An 'aristocratic' poet understands this virtue. In 'September 1913', Yeats's poem on the Dublin Lock-out, he describes the Irish petitebourgeoisie in terms that Aquinas would immediately have understood—these are the people without *magnificentia*:

> What need you, being come to sense,
> But fumble in a greasy till
> And add the halfpence to the pence
> And prayer to shivering prayer, until
> You have dried the marrow from the bone;
> For men were born to pray and save:
> Romantic Ireland's dead and gone,
> It's with O'Leary in the grave.

These Yeats contrasts with the past heroes of the resistance: 'They weighed so lightly what they gave'. That is *magnificentia*.

TEMPERANTIA (TEMPERATENESS)

As courage is the virtue by which our aggression is reasonable, so temperateness is the virtue by which we are reasonable in our sensual desires.

Temperateness is concerned with what is pleasurable, sensually desirable—especially, Aquinas says, from the sense of touch. But it is not, he insists, a matter of regulating the amount of *pleasure* we have. It is not that we should have only a moderate amount of pleasure but that the pleasure we take should lead us to doing the right thing, and what the right thing is is decided by the needs of our bodily life. In other words the 'mean' with which this virtue is concerned is not a mean between excess and defect of pleasure, but a mean between having too much drink or too little, between not having sexual relations when we should and having them when we shouldn't. It is a matter of integrating the pleasures of sensation into a complete life-story.

Although when he discusses intemperance the first vice Aquinas considers is *insensibilitas*, failing in *temperantia* through dislike or fear of pleasure, he admits that most people fail in temperance the opposite way; just as more people are cowardly than are rash, so more people are self-indulgent than are inhibited, cold, and unfeeling. So the business of acquiring temperateness is more usually a matter of restraining appetite than encouraging it. Here too, however, education cannot consist solely of negative prohibitions: it is more fruitful to make the good attractive than to make the bad repulsive. Aquinas quotes with approval Augustine's remark that 'if the mind be lifted up to spiritual things, the *impetus*, pressure, of sensual desire is broken and gradually done away with'. I think for 'spiritual things' you might read 'interesting things', things that engage the mind in some way. Boredom is one of the great enemies of temperateness.

The criterion, then, the 'mean' for temperateness, is decided by our bodily needs, fixed, as Aquinas says, by the order of nature, and the paradigm cases of temperateness concern human survival: the survival of the *individual*, which depends on food and drink and needs a strong appetite for them, and the survival of the *genes*, the human species, which requires a strong sexual appetite. Temperateness is concerned that these appetites do the job they have in our whole complex lives, that the pleasures we take in satisfying them occur in the whole human context to which they naturally belong and are not simply reduced to toys. So, to eat or drink in such a way as to endanger your health and survival is intemperate if you do so *for the sake of the pleasure involved*. You might do it for other reasons, for example to commit suicide (you might glumly drink yourself to death), in which case it would not primarily be intemperate but *unjust* (for your life belongs to society as well as to you). You might also do it for some *good* reason, for there are more important aims in life than health or even individual survival. Intemperateness concerns what is *objectively* the wrong kind of eating and drinking *done for the sake of pleasure.* And similar considerations apply to sex. Sexual activities engaged in for the sake of sheer sensational pleasure which endanger the survival of the species would be intemperate. Thus Aquinas's case against promiscuity is that it endangers society, and hence the species, by not providing through marriage for the child that might be born. For him a marriage would be defective and bad if it did not involve *fidelitas* and personal love between husband and wife. But the *raison d'être* of marriage is children.

It is important to see that the order of nature (the way things are with human animals—we need to eat and reproduce in a human way) determines the correct *behaviour* in these matters; it does not have to determine our immediate motives for action. Thus I can perfectly reasonably and temperately say I am eating this ice cream because I enjoy it; I do not have to be telling myself how good it is for me. But I could do so if asked. I am only intemperate if I simply don't *care* whether it is good for me or not, as would be shown by my continuing to eat it for the sake of pleasure even if I thought it to be seriously bad for me. Similarly, Aquinas says that the reasons that make sexual activity in marriage good and, when informed by grace, *meritorious* for eternal life are desire for children and giving what is owed to (expressing your love for) your partner. Again he does not mean that you cannot reasonably say I am doing this for the fun of it or for the pleasure involved. He means that it would be intemperate to do it for pleasure if you had no concern at all for children or for your partner—if, for example, you would go through with it even though you knew that your partner hated it. What he is condemning here is what is now called marital rape.[5]

When considering fornication, Aquinas brings the upbringing of children into the natural order in which sex is involved, but he also sometimes speaks of sexual intercourse itself as though it has a natural order itself in abstraction from the

[5] Cf. *Summa Theologiae*, Supplement, q. 49.

welfare of a family. On these grounds he makes a case against contraception as preventing the sexual act from having its own procreative function. I do not myself think that it is departing from Aquinas's principles to argue that within the total context of the natural order of the family, the aim of which is not fertility but the upbringing and welfare of children, infertile sex could have its place, for example by spacing pregnancies, as with those species we now know of in which the female after intercourse controls the implantation of the ovum, and only allows it when conditions are suitable; but Aquinas himself certainly does not take this line.

In general Aquinas's treatment of sex is attractively cool and unworried and in strong contrast with a great deal of Christian writing on the topic before and since his time. He insists against a long Augustinian tradition that sexual activity is not sinful because the pleasure is so vehement that it 'suspends the use of reason'. He remarks that if suspending the use of reason were sinful we should never go to sleep. It is acting *contrary* to what is reasonable that makes for sin, not absence of reasoning. On the other hand he has no trace of the individualist view which sees the whole thing in terms of the 'personal fulfilment' of two people who have found each other in love, still less of the view that sex is simply the most enjoyable indoor game. He keeps it, as he does the matter of every human virtue, in its social context. For him the virtue of temperateness is in the end about the kind of emotional balance needed in being good at friendship, the foundation of human community and thus of human life, and part of what he calls *justitia generalis*, 'justice in the broadest sense'.

Evidently there is a great deal to say in detail about temperateness but I'd simply like to quote what he has to say about that constituent of temperateness that he calls a sense of honourableness, which he says is a concern for beauty:

Beauty or handsomeness arises when fine proportions and clarity [brightness] run together. As Dionysius says: God is called Beautiful because he is the source of the harmony and clarity of the universe. So beauty of body consists in well-proportioned limbs and features having a certain clarity [glow] of colour. So also beauty of spirit consists in conversation and actions that are well-formed and suffused with intelligence. This is what we mean by the honourable, which we have identified with the virtuous or the tempering of human affairs by intelligence ... so a sense of honour belongs especially to temperateness which eliminates what is most unseemly and ugly in human beings, namely sheer unbridled self-indulgence (*brutales voluptates*).[6]

This I think gives us a clue to how Aquinas himself envisaged the sensual virtues: they are concerned with a certain sensitivity and gracefulness in our bodily activity so that the community of friends which is the *polis* and, at another level, the *family* consists of people who are not only *just*, wishing equality to each other, but also pleasing to each other in all their gestures and behaviour, a community which is not only fair and caring but also emotionally satisfying.

---

[6] *Summa Theologiae*, 2a2ae, 145, 2.

Index

Index

Index